How AI

Shapes Our Days

Raúl A.S Reynoso

First Edition

2025 Reynoso, Raúl

How AI Shapes Our Days / Raúl Reynoso, - Independent: Amazon Kindle, 138 p.; 23 x 15 cm — (Essay Collection)

ISBN 979-8-3068-3978-3

1. Artificial Intelligence
2. 2. Digital Transformation - 21st Century
3. 3. Digital Humanities I. Ser. Il. t.

Worldwide Distribution

This work was independently published and is available on the Amazon Kindle platform.

www.amazon.com

ISBN 979-8-3068-3978-3 (Independent)

Library of Congress Control Number: 2025900644

Derechos de autor registrados en Safe Creative: 2501210686384
Fecha de registro: 21 de enero de 2025
Más información en: https://www.safecreative.org/work/2501210686384

Printed from amazon

How AI Shapes Our Days

DEDICATION

To all the curious minds who dare to explore the frontier between humanity and technology, and to those who see in artificial intelligence not just an advancement, but an open door to a future full of possibilities. This book is for you.

CONTENTS

ACKNOWLEDGMENTS

I owe sincere gratitude to everyone who contributed, directly or indirectly, to the creation of *How AI Shapes Our Days*. My family has been a pillar of support, giving me the freedom to dive deep into innovative ideas and patiently enduring my late-night brainstorming sessions.

I also want to recognize the colleagues and friends in the AI field who challenged my assumptions, shared their ability, and pushed me to refine each chapter. Their real-world experience shaped much of what's on these pages.

A special thank-you goes to my editor and beta readers, whose insightful critiques and keen diligence elevated this work.

Finally, I'm grateful for the global community of AI pioneers—researchers, developers, entrepreneurs, and enthusiasts—whose breakthroughs spark progress in ways we can only begin to imagine. Without their passion and dedication, this book would not exist.

How AI Shapes Our Days

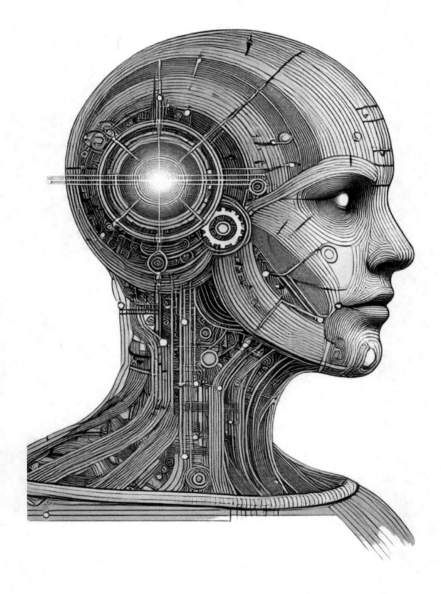

1 CHAPTER:

INTRODUCTION: A WORLD REWRITTEN BY ALGORITHMS

The Dawn of a New Era

Artificial Intelligence (AI) is no longer the stuff of science fiction. It's here, intricately woven into the fabric of our daily lives, shaping how we work, play, and connect with one another. From the subtle convenience of a voice-activated assistant to the profound implications of predictive analytics, AI has become both a silent observer and an active participant in the human journey.

AI's emergence marks a pivotal transformation in history, akin to the Industrial Revolution or the advent of the internet. With capabilities ranging from natural language processing to image recognition, AI systems are designed to mimic and, at times, surpass human intelligence. This unprecedented growth raises questions about its influence: How does it empower us? How does it challenge our autonomy? These inquiries form the backbone of this book, aiming to illuminate AI's pervasive presence.

Artificial Intelligence (AI) has become more than a technological breakthrough; it is a profound shift in the way humanity interacts with the world. To truly grasp its significance, one must look beyond the algorithms and codes to see the intricate web of influence AI has spun around us. This is not just the dawn of a new era but the awakening of a paradigm where machines and humans coalesce into an unprecedented symphony of possibility.

At its core, this era stands for a departure from linear progression into exponential growth. Traditional inventions often solved specific problems, but AI offers something more—a dynamic, evolving entity that learns, adapts, and predicts. It's as if humanity has crafted a tool that doesn't merely obey but collaborates, anticipating needs we haven't yet articulated.

Consider the invisible hand of AI in daily life: the voice assistant that not only reminds you of your appointments but adjusts your schedule based on traffic patterns, or the email filter that instinctively separates priority messages from distractions. These innovations, while subtle, epitomize the dawn of an era where AI shapes our surroundings with almost intuitive precision.

Yet, this new dawn is not merely technological. It is philosophical and existential. As AI takes on roles that were once the exclusive domain of human cognition, we are compelled to redefine concepts like intelligence, creativity, and even consciousness. Can a machine utterly understand us, or does it simply mimic understanding? And if the mimicry is indistinguishable from the real, does it matter?

This chapter explores the profound questions born of this transformation. The dawn of AI's era challenges us to confront our own limitations and aspirations. It invites us to embrace a future where intelligence is no longer confined to the human mind but shared across networks, devices, and systems. It's a redefinition of progress—not as a solitary journey but as a collaborative evolution.

This evolution, however, is not without its shadows. The marvel of AI's precision is counterbalanced by its opacity. How do algorithms decide what they decide? Can we, as creators, remain in control of creations that surpass our understanding? These questions form the heart of this new dawn—a time as exhilarating as it is daunting, filled with opportunities to uplift and risks to navigate.

The dawn of this era is a call to responsibility. As we advance, we must remember that AI reflects our own intentions, values, and biases. It is a mirror as much as it is a tool, showing us who we are and what we prioritize. The challenge is to ensure that this reflection is one we can be proud of—a testament to human ingenuity, guided by ethics and driven by the desire to enhance rather than diminish our collective experience.

Beneath the surface of this transformative age lies an unseen momentum—the silent workings of algorithms that orchestrate the rhythms of modern life. These systems, powered by machine learning, analyze vast amounts of data to discern patterns and predict outcomes. Their influence extends from perfecting supply chains to fine-tuning weather forecasts, making them indispensable in sectors as diverse as agriculture, finance, and healthcare.

This momentum, however, is not without its intricacies. AI's ability to process information at an unprecedented scale introduces ethical dilemmas. For instance, when predictive models guide hiring decisions or distribute medical resources, how do we ensure fairness and transparency? The challenge lies in balancing efficiency with equity, ensuring that AI serves as an instrument of progress rather than perpetuating existing inequities.

Moreover, the pace of AI's evolution demands a reimagining of education and skill development. As traditional job roles are augmented or replaced by automation, the need for adaptability becomes paramount. Workers must cultivate not only technical ability but also critical thinking and emotional intelligence—skills that complement rather than compete with AI.

The unseen momentum of AI also invites us to reconsider the boundaries of human creativity. With algorithms capable of composing music, generating artwork, and writing prose, the line between human and machine artistry becomes increasingly blurred. While some view this as a threat to originality, others see it as an opportunity for collaboration, where human imagination and machine precision converge to create new forms of expression.

As this chapter unfolds, it becomes clear that the dawn of AI's era is both a gift and a challenge. It offers tools to elevate human potential while demanding vigilance to mitigate its pitfalls. By embracing this duality, we can navigate the complexities of this transformative age with wisdom and foresight.

Recent advancements have proved AI's ability to enhance human creativity. For instance, AI-powered tools can help artists in generating novel ideas, offering new perspectives that might not appear through traditional methods. This symbiosis allows creators to explore uncharted territories, pushing the boundaries of their craft. (Gorilla, 2024)

However, this collaboration is not without its complexities. The integration of AI into creative processes needs a reevaluation of authorship and originality. When an AI system contributes to a piece of art or literature, questions arise: Who holds the creative ownership? Is the work a product of human ingenuity, machine computation, or an amalgamation of both? These inquiries challenge our traditional understanding of creativity, urging us to redefine it in the context of human-AI collaboration.

Moreover, the influence of AI extends beyond individual creativity to societal norms and ethical considerations. The deployment of AI in various sectors, from healthcare to entertainment, reflects and amplifies human values and biases. It's crucial to ensure that AI systems are designed and implemented with ethical guidelines that promote fairness and inclusivity. As one article notes, "AI reflects our own intentions, values, and biases. It is a mirror as much as it is a tool, showing us who we are and what we prioritize." Forbes

In this new era, the relationship between humans and AI is characterized by a dynamic interplay of augmentation and adaptation. AI systems can process vast amounts of data, finding patterns and insights that inform human decision-making. This capability enhances our cognitive functions, enabling more informed and efficient choices. However, it also requires us to adapt, developing new skills and competencies to effectively collaborate with AI. As highlighted in a recent study, "AI introduces a qualitative shift in cognition, akin to a transition from classical to quantum computing." Psychology Hoy

As we continue to explore the implications of AI's integration into our lives, it's essential to approach this transformation with a sense of responsibility and ethical consideration. By fostering a collaborative relationship with AI, we can harness its potential to enhance human creativity and cognition, while ensuring that it serves to uplift and empower humanity.

Understanding the Role of AI in Everyday Life

What was once limited to experimental labs has now found its way into every corner of modern society. AI curates the news we consume, recommends the songs we love, and even predicts the next item we might buy online. While these conveniences may seem trivial, their cumulative effect reshapes habits, preferences, and decision-making processes.

Take, for instance, the algorithms powering streaming platforms. They analyze viewing patterns to suggest content, transforming passive consumption into an interactive experience. Similarly, AI-driven navigation apps adapt in real-time, improving routes based on traffic and user behavior. These examples underline how AI enriches daily routines while subtly steering our choices.

However, the power of AI to personalize experiences comes with deeper implications. The same tools that recommend your next favorite show can also limit your exposure to diverse perspectives. By tailoring content to individual preferences, algorithms may inadvertently create "bubbles" where users are only exposed to information that aligns with their existing beliefs. This phenomenon, often referred to as "echo chambers," can reinforce biases and polarize opinions, a significant concern in the context of news consumption and social discourse.

Moreover, AI doesn't operate in a vacuum. Its decisions and recommendations are rooted in data—data that reflects human behavior, history, and, inevitably, human biases. If a hiring algorithm favors certain candidates over others or a predictive policing tool disproportionately targets specific communities, the issue isn't just technological but deeply societal. It forces us to confront the uncomfortable reality that AI often amplifies the flaws in the data it's fed.

Beyond the individual, AI's influence seeps into the fabric of society, shaping cultural norms and influencing collective consciousness. Social media platforms, driven by AI algorithms, play a pivotal role in finding what stories gain traction and which voices are amplified. While this democratization of information can empower marginalized groups, it also poses risks, such as the spread of misinformation and the erosion of privacy. The balance between these outcomes depends on how AI systems are designed and governed.

AI's reach extends into the workplace, where it drives decisions that affect productivity and organizational culture. For example, AI-powered tools can show inefficiencies or predict market trends, giving businesses a competitive edge. However, these benefits come with the risk of dehumanizing workflows, as decisions based solely on data may overlook the nuances of human behavior and the importance of empathy in leadership.

Education, too, is undergoing a quiet revolution. AI is increasingly used to personalize learning experiences, adapting to students' unique needs and pacing. While this holds the promise of bridging educational gaps, it also raises questions about dependency and the diminishing role of human educators. Can a machine truly inspire creativity or empathy in the same way a teacher can? These are the ethical crossroads we must navigate as AI becomes an integral part of our lives.

In this complex landscape, our relationship with AI evolves daily. It's no longer a question of man versus machine but of partnership—a symbiotic relationship where each shapes the other. We teach AI through our interactions, preferences, and feedback, and in return, AI adapts to better serve our needs. This mutual influence underscores the need for conscious engagement. As users, we must remain vigilant, questioning the motivations behind AI-driven suggestions and resisting the temptation to passively accept them.

As we navigate this AI-dominated landscape, one truth appears:

technology reflects its creators. The ethical dilemmas and societal impacts tied to AI are not inherent to the machines but arise from human decisions—from the priorities we set during its development to the values we embed in its programming. Recognizing this is the first step toward ensuring that AI not only augments human potential but also aligns with our aspirations for a fair and fair world.

Understanding the role of AI in our daily lives is more than just analyzing its functionalities; it's about reflecting on its broader implications. How we choose to interact with and shape these technologies will define the trajectory of this era, deciding whether it becomes a beacon of progress or a cautionary tale of overreach and neglect.

The realm of creativity has always been seen as uniquely human—a domain where imagination, emotion, and personal experience converge to produce art, literature, and ideas. However, the rise of AI in content creation is challenging this notion, particularly in the sphere of writing. Today, it's entirely feasible for an AI to generate a book, from conceptualization to final draft, using advanced natural language processing models. While this might sound revolutionary, it also raises questions about authenticity, purpose, and the future of creative expression.

Consider this very book. Could an AI have written it? On the surface, the answer might seem plausible. After all, AI systems can generate coherent, well-structured narratives, synthesizing information from vast databases, and even mimicking stylistic nuances. But the deeper essence of this work lies in its intent and its reflection of a human perspective. Writing, at its core, is not just about assembling words; it's about conveying ideas, emotions, and a worldview. An AI might replicate structure, but can it truly replicate substance?

The growing trend of using AI to help in creating books stems from the accessibility and efficiency it offers. Aspiring authors can use AI tools to outline their ideas, generate drafts, or even enhance their prose. This has democratized the publishing world, enabling voices that might otherwise have gone unheard to find an audience. Yet, this also leads to a saturation of the market with content that, while polished, may lack depth or originality.

Moreover, the economic motivations behind AI-driven writing cannot be ignored. Publishing houses and independent authors alike recognize the cost-saving potential of AI. A machine doesn't require rest, compensation, or creative breaks. It can churn out content at a pace no human could match, aligning perfectly with a market that thrives on volume and speed. This industrialization of creativity, however, risks undermining the value of authentic, labor-intensive storytelling.

For readers, the distinction between AI-generated and human-authored works might blur. How can one differentiate a novel born of human experience from one sculpted by algorithms? And does it even matter if the narrative resonates? These questions reflect the evolving dynamics of creativity in the age of AI, where the lines between innovation and imitation are increasingly indistinct.

This chapter invites readers to ponder the implications of AI's role in literature and the broader creative industries. While the technology offers remarkable tools for inspiration and productivity, it also challenges us to safeguard the integrity of human expression. The ability to create is not just a technical skill but a deeply human endeavor, imbued with values, struggles, and aspirations that no machine can fully replicate.

2 CHAPTER:

MORNING RITUALS: AI'S GENTLE AWAKENING

Mornings have always felt sacred to me, a quiet threshold between the chaos of sleep and the demands of the day. It's in those first moments, when the world outside still seems half-asleep, that I've noticed how deeply technology has woven itself into my routine. The soft chime of my alarm clock doesn't just wake me—it adjusts itself to my sleep patterns, learning when to rouse me for optimal energy. It's subtle, almost imperceptible, yet it sets the tone for everything that follows.

I remember when mornings were dictated by rigid schedules and blaring alarms, where the jarring buzz of a clock would yank me out of dreams. Now, my mornings feel more curated, as if technology understands that the beginning of the day isn't just functional—it's emotional. My alarm is no longer just a sound but a guide, synchronizing with my calendar to remind me of the commitments ahead. Sometimes it even suggests an earlier wake-up time, factoring in weather changes or unexpected traffic delays.

The way AI integrates into my mornings isn't limited to alarms. There's something reassuring about how it anticipates my needs, like the smart assistant that greets me with a brief rundown of the day. It tells me the weather, my first meeting, and whether I need to carry an umbrella. It's efficient, yes, but it's also personal, as though it's not just feeding me information but helping me prepare emotionally for what's to come.

This subtle orchestration extends into my breakfast routine. I've always been someone who forgets to stock the fridge, but now, AI-powered grocery apps track what I consume and suggest when to restock. They even recommend recipes based on what's available, turning a mundane decision into something creative. Sometimes, it feels like these small conveniences free up mental space for the bigger tasks of the day.

I often wonder how we reached this point—where technology has become so integrated into something as personal as a morning. It's not just about efficiency; it's about creating an experience that feels supportive, almost human. There's a certain irony in that, isn't there? Machines, devoid of feelings, designing mornings that feel warm and intentional.

There is also a trust I've had to build with this technology. Allowing a device to track my sleep, analyze my habits, and even make decisions for me required a shift in mindset. It was not easy at first. I questioned what I might be giving up in exchange for these comforts—my data, my autonomy. Over time, though, I realized that these tools are not about taking over but complementing the life I already live. They do not replace my judgment; they refine it.

Still, there's a line I've chosen to draw. While I rely on AI for guidance, I've made it a point to keep certain rituals untouched. The way I savor my morning coffee, for instance, stays deliberately analog—a moment to ground myself amidst all the digital interactions. It's in these small acts of defiance that I remind myself of what mornings used to be, and what they still can be.

Smart Alarms and Personalized Schedules

Imagine waking up each day to a rhythm crafted uniquely for you, a tempo that resonates with your internal clock rather than the rigid chime of a one-size-fits-all alarm. Smart alarms are no longer mere devices; they are companions attuned to our sleep cycles, energy patterns, and daily ambitions. They orchestrate mornings that feel less like a jolt and more like a seamless transition from rest to action.

Gone are the days when alarms were intrusive. Today, they analyze sleep stages, gently waking you during a light phase, ensuring you feel rested rather than disoriented. But the ingenuity doesn't end there. These alarms synchronize with your personal goals and routines, adapting as your priorities shift. For instance, an alarm might wake you earlier on days requiring extra preparation while granting added rest on quieter mornings.

Beyond the awakening process, smart systems extend their reach into the architecture of our schedules. Personalized planning tools integrate seamlessly with alarms, tailoring your day with precision. They account for factors like traffic patterns, weather forecasts, and even your productivity peaks, crafting a timeline that prioritizes efficiency without sacrificing balance.

Consider a day shaped not by the tyranny of the clock but by an organic flow—your most crucial tasks tackled during your mental prime, with breaks perfectly timed to rejuvenate rather than disrupt. These systems do more than distribute hours; they curate moments, blending work, leisure, and rest into a harmonious cadence.

This evolution in time management challenges our traditional notions of productivity. No longer is success measured by the sheer volume of tasks completed but by the alignment of those tasks with your natural rhythm and aspirations. In this landscape, individuals are not slaves to schedules but architects of their own time, empowered by tools that adapt to their uniqueness.

Smart alarms and personalized schedules stand for more than technological advances; they symbolize a shift in how we perceive time and its management. They teach us that efficiency is not about doing more but about doing better—with intention, focus, and a touch of humanity woven into the fabric of our days.

The growing integration of smart alarms and personalized schedules into daily life signals a transformation not just in technology but in how individuals perceive time management. At the forefront of this evolution are companies that are using advanced algorithms, AI, and data analytics to craft tools that seamlessly adapt to individual lifestyles.

Sleep Cycle, for instance, stands as a trailblazer in smart alarm technology. Their platform analyzes sleep patterns to awaken users during light sleep phases, promoting a refreshed state of mind. By incorporating user data and feedback, Sleep Cycle's offerings go beyond alarms, creating a personalized morning routine that improves energy levels.

Google, with its expansive ecosystem, is redefining scheduling through its calendar and AI assistant services. By analyzing even downtime. The integration of predictive algorithms ensures schedules are not static but dynamic, adapting to real-time changes in priorities or unforeseen disruptions.

Similarly, **Withing´s** has merged health tracking with smart alarm technology. Their devices check physiological data like heart rate and breathing patterns, using this information to fine-tune wake-up times. This comprehensive approach ensures users' mornings align with their overall wellness goals, fostering a balance between rest and activity.

Apple has also made significant strides in this realm. The Sleep app, designed for use with the Apple Watch, provides detailed analytics on sleep quality while offering recommendations to enhance daily routines. Its seamless integration with the broader Apple ecosystem creates a comprehensive environment where time management feels intuitive rather than imposed.

Microsoft is using its ability in AI to develop smart scheduling tools within Outlook. These features prioritize tasks, recommend best times for meetings, and block focus periods, ensuring a balanced workload. Microsoft's approach highlights the importance of aligning professional productivity with personal well-being.

Emerging startups are also entering this space, pushing the boundaries of what smart alarms and personalized schedules can achieve. Companies like **Rise Science** focus on sleep optimization for high-performance individuals, providing insights and actionable strategies to enhance rest and productivity.

These innovators prove that the future of time management lies in personalization. By tailoring schedules and routines to the unique rhythms of everyone, these tools empower users to reclaim control over their days, making every moment purposeful and aligned with their aspirations.

The Seamless Integration of AI into Our Mornings

Mornings have long been regarded as the most crucial part of the day. They set the tone for productivity, energy, and mood. With the advent of artificial intelligence, our mornings are transforming from chaotic beginnings to well-orchestrated routines that blend convenience, efficiency, and personalization.

A Personalized Wake-Up Call: Gone are the days when alarm clocks jolted us awake with a generic buzz. AI-powered systems like smart speakers and virtual assistants now analyze our sleep patterns through wearable devices or smart mattresses. These systems decide the best time to wake us, ensuring we rise feeling refreshed. The alarm is no longer a one-size-fits-all experience but a tailored start to the day, with options ranging from soothing music to motivational affirmations based on the user's preferences.

Curating Morning Information

AI has mastered the art of delivering relevant information right when we need it. Imagine waking up to a briefing designed specifically for you: weather updates tailored to your location, the latest news aligned with your interests, and traffic reports for your morning commute. These insights, delivered seamlessly through AI, empower us to make informed decisions before even leaving bed.

Breakfast, Simplified

For many, deciding what to eat in the morning can be a challenge. AI-driven kitchen devices have revolutionized this process. Smart fridges track inventory, suggest recipes based on available ingredients, and even accommodate dietary restrictions. Some systems go a step further, synchronizing with grocery delivery apps to ensure your pantry is always stocked. Preparing a nutritious breakfast has never been easier or more efficient.

Streamlining Grooming Routines

AI-enhanced mirrors and personal care devices are reshaping how we prepare for the day. Smart mirrors offer grooming tips, skincare recommendations, and even outfit suggestions based on weather conditions and upcoming events in your calendar. AI-powered toothbrushes and razors track usage and provide real-time feedback, ensuring best hygiene and care.

Morning Workouts, Tailored to You

Exercise routines have also benefited immensely from AI's integration. Fitness apps and devices create dynamic workout plans based on individual fitness goals, health data, and even sleep quality from the night before. Virtual trainers offer guidance and motivation, making personalized fitness accessible to everyone, no matter their location or schedule.

Mental Wellness Through AI

Mindfulness and mental wellness are vital for a balanced start to the day. AI-driven apps offer meditation sessions, breathing exercises, and mood trackers tailored to your emotional state. By analyzing voice tone, facial expressions, or user input, these systems adjust recommendations to provide the most effective mental health practices for the individual.

Seamless Transition to Productivity

As we step out the door or settle into our home office, AI continues to pave the way for productivity. Smart assistants remind us of appointments, prepare our to-do lists, and synchronize with other devices to ensure our day starts smoothly. This interconnected ecosystem drops stress and allows us to focus on what truly matters.

The Human Touch Amid Automation

While AI has undeniably perfected our mornings, it is crucial to strike a balance between automation and human connection. Sharing a cup of coffee with loved ones or taking a moment to enjoy the sunrise can ground us, reminding us of the simplicity and beauty of life beyond technology.

AI's integration into our mornings is not just about efficiency; it's about creating space for what truly enriches our lives. By offloading mundane tasks to intelligent systems, we can reclaim moments for self-care, connection, and purpose. As AI continues to evolve, our mornings are becoming a harmonious blend of technology and humanity, setting the stage for brighter and more fulfilling days ahead.

The integration of artificial intelligence into our mornings doesn't stop at home—it extends to the journey that bridges our personal lives and professional commitments. The commute, once considered a mundane or even stressful part of the day, is being reimagined by AI to create a seamless, efficient, and even enjoyable experience. This transformation is particularly clear in how vehicles—our trusted companions on the road—are becoming smarter, safer, and more in tune with our needs.

Smart Navigation for Smarter Routes

AI-powered navigation systems like Google Maps and Waze have already revolutionized how we travel by predicting traffic patterns, suggesting alternative routes, and providing real-time updates. But these systems are evolving further, using predictive analytics to predict road conditions even before we leave home. By analyzing historical data, weather conditions, and live traffic feeds, AI systems now propose the most efficient route with an unprecedented level of accuracy.

For professionals, this means not only shorter commutes but also the ability to plan their time effectively. Arriving at work on time becomes a certainty rather than a gamble, reducing the stress associated with unpredictable traffic delays.

The Rise of Autonomous Vehicles

Self-driving cars are at the forefront of AI integration in transportation. These vehicles are equipped with advanced sensors, cameras, and algorithms that enable them to navigate roads autonomously. The implications for morning commutes are profound:

- **Safety First**: AI-driven systems drop human errors, which account for most accidents. Features like automatic braking, lane-keeping aid, and collision avoidance ensure safer journeys.

- **Enhanced Productivity**: With the car managing the driving, commuters can use their time more effectively. Reading, responding to emails, or even taking part in virtual meetings becomes a possibility, turning travel time into productive hours.

- **Stress-Free Travel**: Autonomous vehicles end the frustrations of driving in traffic, allowing passengers to relax, meditate, or enjoy entertainment.

Vehicle Personalization and Comfort

AI has made vehicles not just modes of transportation but personalized spaces. Imagine a car that adjusts its interior temperature, seat settings, and ambient lighting based on your preferences before you step in. AI systems can even play your favorite podcast or music playlist, setting the tone for your day.

Additionally, smart vehicles are integrating with personal assistants like Amazon Alexa or Google Assistant, allowing users to control their cars remotely. Need to warm up your car on a chilly morning? Simply ask your virtual assistant to manage it while you finish your coffee.

Carpooling and Shared Mobility

AI is also driving the growth of shared mobility services. Ride-hailing platforms like Uber and Lyft, powered by AI algorithms, optimize carpooling by matching riders traveling in similar directions. This not only reduces costs for users but also minimizes the number of vehicles on the road, contributing to reduced traffic congestion and a lower carbon footprint.

Autonomous ride-sharing fleets are on the horizon, promising even greater efficiency. These vehicles can be summoned on demand, work 24/7, and dynamically adjust their routes to accommodate multiple passengers without delays.

AI-Driven Sustainability

Sustainability is a key concern in modern transportation, and AI is playing a pivotal role in addressing it. Electric vehicles (EVs) are becoming increasingly popular, and AI systems refine their performance in several ways:

- **Battery Management**: AI monitors battery health, perfects charging schedules, and finds the most efficient charging stations along your route.
- **Eco-Friendly Routing**: Navigation systems can calculate routes that minimize fuel consumption or energy usage, promoting greener commutes.

Governments and companies are also adopting AI-powered solutions to create smart city infrastructures, such as traffic lights that adapt to real-time conditions, reducing idling and emissions during peak hours.

AI in Public Transportation

For those who prefer public transport, AI is enhancing efficiency and reliability. Real-time updates on bus and train schedules, AI-predicted delays, and mobile ticketing systems are improving the commuting experience. In the future, autonomous buses and trains could further streamline public transit, making it a more attractive choice for urban commuters.

Building a Positive Emotional Connection

AI's integration into morning commutes goes beyond convenience and efficiency—it has the potential to improve our emotional well-being. By reducing stressors such as traffic jams and the unpredictability of travel times, AI allows commuters to begin their workdays with a sense of calm and control. Vehicles that interact with passengers through conversational AI, offering uplifting messages or reminders for self-care, can contribute to an overall positive mindset.

The way we commute to work is undergoing a profound transformation thanks to the integration of artificial intelligence into vehicles and the entire transportation ecosystem. Traveling to work is no longer just about reaching a destination; it's becoming an opportunity to enhance our mornings, make our lives easier, and even find moments of enjoyment along the way.

Imagine starting your day without the stress of unexpected traffic jams or the constant worry of being late. AI-driven navigation systems now analyze live traffic data, weather conditions, and even historical patterns to suggest the best routes, saving you time and helping you avoid unnecessary frustration. It's like having a personal assistant who clears your path while you sip your coffee or plan your day ahead.

But it doesn't stop there. Vehicles themselves are becoming smarter, almost like companions that understand and adapt to your needs. Picture this: as you approach your car in the morning, it has already adjusted the seat to your preferred position, set the interior temperature to your liking, and queued up your favorite podcast or music playlist. Instead of feeling rushed or distracted, you're stepping into an environment designed to make you feel comfortable, focused, and ready to take on the day.

For those who spend a lot of time driving, AI is transforming how we use that time. With the rise of autonomous vehicles, commuting is no longer just about driving—it's about making the most of your journey. Autonomous cars can manage the road, allowing you to answer emails, prepare for a meeting, or simply take a moment to relax before diving into the day's tasks. This shift not only saves time but also reduces the mental strain of navigating busy streets or dealing with aggressive drivers.

AI is also bringing us closer to a sustainable future. Electric vehicles, guided by intelligent systems, are now more efficient than ever. These systems manage battery performance, find the nearest charging stations, and suggest eco-friendly routes that reduce energy consumption. Even for those who don't own a car, AI-powered public transport systems are making commuting smoother. Real-time updates on schedules and delays keep you informed, while autonomous buses and trains are slowly becoming a reality, promising a cleaner and more reliable way to travel.

Shared mobility services like Uber and Lyft are also getting a boost from AI. By connecting people traveling in the same direction, these platforms not only reduce the cost of commuting but also decrease the number of vehicles on the road. This means less traffic and a smaller environmental impact—benefits that everyone can appreciate.

What's truly exciting is how AI is making commutes feel less like a chore and more like a valuable part of the day. Whether it's reducing the stress of driving, giving you time to prepare mentally for work, or even creating moments of peace, AI is reshaping the emotional experience of traveling to work. Vehicles are evolving into spaces where we can find balance—offering a chance to breathe, reflect, or connect with loved ones via a quick call, all while the car manages the road.

As AI continues to advance, it's helping us reimagine the way we approach mornings and commutes. It's no longer just about transportation; it's about creating a journey that aligns with our needs and values. From making our lives more convenient to fostering a connection with the world around us, AI is turning every mile into a symbol of progress, sustainability, and humanity.

In the end, the seamless integration of AI into our mornings and commutes is a testament to how technology can enhance the simplest yet most important parts of our daily lives. It's no longer just about waking up and getting from point A to point B—it's about creating a morning that flows effortlessly, freeing us to focus on what truly matters. From personalized wake-up routines to smart navigation and autonomous vehicles, AI is transforming the mundane into the extraordinary, infusing each moment with intention, convenience, and innovation.

This isn't just a technological revolution; it's a human one. AI predicts our needs, simplifies our choices, and gives us back time—time to breathe, to connect, to prepare. Whether it's a car that learns your preferences, a route optimized to save both minutes and stress, or a virtual assistant aligning your schedule with precision, AI is shaping mornings that feel more in tune with who we are and what we value.

As we continue to embrace this evolution, mornings will no longer be a rush of tasks but a harmonious start to the day, where every element works together seamlessly. The technology driving these changes isn't just about gadgets and algorithms; it's about crafting a life where efficiency meets humanity. It's about using innovation to reclaim time, reduce stress, and build a future where the journey—whether it's through your morning routine or your commute—is just as meaningful as the destination.

"AI doesn't just evolve; it redefines how we live, connect, and dream."

3 CHAPTER

NAVIGATING THE DAY: AI AS A CO-PILOT

In the fast-paced rhythm of modern life, managing tasks, responsibilities, and priorities can want to pilot a complex journey. This is where artificial intelligence steps in—not as a replacement for human effort, but as a reliable co-pilot, guiding us through the day with precision, adaptability, and support. From morning to night, AI seamlessly integrates into our routines, helping us navigate with confidence and clarity.

Starting the Day with Purpose, the role of AI begins the moment we wake up. Personalized virtual assistants like Siri, Alexa, or Google Assistant function as co-pilots for our mornings, providing weather updates, reminders, and a curated overview of the day ahead. By synchronizing with calendars and other applications, AI ensures that nothing important slips through the cracks. Instead of starting the day overwhelmed, we are equipped with a clear roadmap.

For example, imagine waking up to an AI-generated schedule that not only lists meetings and deadlines but also suggests best times for breaks, exercise, and focus work based on your past habits. This initiative-taking help transforms mornings from a chaotic rush into an organized and mindful beginning.

Streamlining Workflows ss we step into our professional roles; AI becomes an indispensable partner in navigating the complexities of work. Intelligent tools now manage emails, prioritize tasks, and even automate repetitive processes. By analyzing patterns in communication and project timelines, AI systems can name what requires immediate attention and what can wait, helping us focus on high-impact activities.

In industries ranging from finance to healthcare to creative fields, AI acts as a co-pilot by offering insights that were previously unimaginable. For instance:

- **Creative industries:** AI-powered tools generate design prototypes or help with content creation, leaving professionals more time to focus on ideation and refinement.
- **Healthcare:** AI systems analyze patient data to provide doctors with diagnostics or treatment options in record time.
- **Business and finance:** AI evaluates market trends, improves budgets, and forecasts outcomes, enabling faster, smarter decision-making.

Navigating the Unexpected one of AI's most remarkable abilities is its adaptability in the face of change. Life is unpredictable meetings run late, traffic patterns shift, or unexpected challenges arise. AI systems excel at recalibrating on the fly, offering alternative solutions, rescheduling events, or suggesting ways to recover lost time. For example, a smart assistant can suggest a new route home to avoid sudden traffic or reorganize your work priorities after an urgent task appears.

By serving as a responsive co-pilot, AI reduces stress and creates a sense of control, even in chaotic moments.

AI in Personal Life: Outside of work, AI continues to guide us. Whether it's managing household tasks, assisting with meal planning, or helping with financial management, AI systems act as co-pilots in our personal lives. Smart home devices can automatically adjust lighting and temperature based on preferences or time of day, while fitness apps create personalized workout plans and track progress over time.

Even social connections receive help from AI's influence. Recommendation algorithms suggest new books, movies, or experiences based on our interests, ensuring our leisure time is spent on activities that truly resonate with us.

Fostering Balance and Well-Being a true co-pilot doesn't just focus on the journey—it ensures the pilot remains in good condition. AI-powered wellness tools help us support balance amid our busy schedules. Meditation apps like Headspace or Calm, powered by AI, offer personalized mindfulness exercises tailored to our emotional state. Health trackers watch physical activity, heart rate, and sleep patterns, providing actionable feedback to improve overall well-being.

By supporting both productivity and self-care, AI encourages an integrated approach to navigating the day.

AI: The Invisible Partner; Perhaps the most remarkable aspect of AI as a co-pilot is its invisibility. It integrates so seamlessly into our lives that its presence often goes unnoticed. From recommending the best time to send an email for maximum impact to suggesting a playlist to match your mood, AI runs in the background, making decisions and solving problems without demanding attention.

This unobtrusive support enables us to focus on what truly matters— our goals, relationships, and passions—while AI oversees the details.

Looking ahead as AI continues to advance, its role as a co-pilot will only become more nuanced and impactful. Emerging technologies like generative AI, predictive analytics, and machine learning are already expanding the possibilities, helping us navigate the complexities of life with greater ease.

AI isn't just about efficiency—it's about empowerment. It allows us to reclaim time, focus on what brings us joy, and handle challenges with confidence. With AI as our co-pilot, we are not simply managing our days; we are mastering them. In this new era, technology isn't leading the way; it's walking beside us, ensuring that we navigate life with purpose, clarity, and balance.

From Virtual Assistants to AI-Powered Productivity Tools

The journey of AI as a co-pilot is perhaps most evident in the tools, we use daily—those that simplify our lives, streamline our work, and elevate our productivity. From virtual assistants managing our schedules to sophisticated AI platforms perfecting complex workflows, these technologies show how deeply AI is woven into the fabric of modern life.

Virtual assistants like Alexa, Siri, Google Assistant, and Cortana have become indispensable companions in our daily routines. These AI-powered tools are no longer limited to answering questions or setting timers; they've evolved into dynamic personal managers.

- **Scheduling Simplified**: Virtual assistants can synchronize multiple calendars, set reminders, and even predict conflicts. They're designed to anticipate your needs, such as reminding you of a meeting location based on traffic conditions or suggesting rescheduling when overlapping events arise.
- **Voice-Activated Ease**: Hands-free interactions enable multitasking. Whether dictating a quick email while preparing breakfast or asking for directions during your commute, virtual assistants keep you on track without interrupting your flow.
- **Smart Home Integration**: By connecting to smart home systems, virtual assistants allow you to control lighting, temperature, and appliances with simple voice commands, creating an environment tailored to your preferences.

These assistants function as the foundation of AI-powered navigation through life, overseeing the mundane so you can focus on more meaningful tasks.

AI-Powered Productivity Platforms

Beyond virtual assistants, specialized AI tools are transforming productivity in more targeted ways. These platforms cater to professionals, students, and creatives alike, helping to refine workflows, spark innovation, and maximize output.

- **Email and Communication Management**: Tools like Grammarly and AI-driven email filters don't just check grammar or prioritize messages—they learn your communication style, adapt to your tone, and even suggest responses. AI is enabling faster, more polished communication.
- **Collaborative Platforms**: AI-enhanced platforms like Slack, Microsoft Teams, and Asana use machine learning to recommend task assignments, find bottlenecks, and prioritize workflows. They refine collaboration, ensuring every team member is aligned.
- **Content Creation**: For writers, marketers, and designers, tools like Canva, Jasper, or even Adobe's AI-enhanced features help create compelling content. These tools can suggest headlines, draft articles, or enhance designs, turning ideas into polished products faster than ever.

AI in Decision-Making and Data Management

In industries driven by data, AI is revolutionizing decision-making. By analyzing large datasets in real time, AI tools show trends, offer actionable insights, and even predict outcomes. For example:

- **Business Strategy**: AI platforms like Tableau and Power BI visualize data in ways that make complex trends easy to understand, enabling faster and more informed decisions.
- **Financial Tools**: AI in personal finance apps, such as Mint or Pocket Smith, helps users budget, forecast expenses, and even automate savings. In corporate finance, AI predicts market trends and assesses risks, empowering businesses to act with confidence.

These tools take the guesswork out of decision-making, enabling users to focus on strategy and execution

AI for Time Optimization

One of the most valuable contributions of AI is its ability to perfect time, ensuring every minute is used effectively. Tools like Rescue Time or Time Doctor analyze how users spend their day, offering insights into productivity patterns. By naming time sinks and suggesting adjustments, AI helps users reclaim hours for what truly matters.

Even more advanced systems, such as predictive scheduling software, adapt to users' energy levels and focus patterns, scheduling high-priority tasks when they're most likely to be effective. This personalized approach to time management ensures that productivity aligns with natural rhythms.

Personalization at Scale

What sets AI-powered productivity tools apart is their ability to personalize at scale. These systems don't just offer blanket solutions—they adapt to individual preferences, learning over time to better suit each user's style and goals. For instance:

- **Creative Inspiration**: AI tools suggest ideas based on past projects, sparking creativity when users hit a mental block.
- **Workstyle Adaptation**: Whether you prefer short bursts of focused work or longer, uninterrupted sessions, AI tools adapt to match your workflow.
- **Initiative-taking Assistance**: Rather than waiting for input, many AI tools proactively suggest solutions, offer shortcuts, or flag potential issues before they arise.

The Future of AI-Driven Productivity

As AI continues to evolve, the line between virtual assistants and productivity tools is blurring. Future systems will integrate even more deeply, acting as comprehensive co-pilots that oversee every aspect of work and life. Imagine a single AI system that:

- Manages your schedule.
- Tracks your health metrics.
- Improves your work projects.
- Provides insights for personal growth.

This emerging vision of seamlessly integrated, AI-enhanced tools carries the potential to transform not only how we organize our tasks but also how we experience our daily lives. These innovations go beyond simplifying workloads—they weave a new rhythm into our routines, one that aligns with both our ambitions and our well-being. By lifting the weight of repetitive chores and fine-tuning the flow of our activities, these systems create space for us to engage more deeply with the moments and connections that give life its meaning.

What makes this shift extraordinary isn't just the technology—it's the deeply human ways in which it complements our lives. These tools don't merely assist; they adapt, learning the subtle nuances of how we think, work, and rest. They offer not just solutions but understanding, turning every interaction into an opportunity for growth. With this kind of support, we're not just completing tasks; we're crafting experiences that reflect who we are and what we value most.

In this landscape, AI ceases to be a static tool. It becomes a living presence in our day, guiding with precision yet leaving room for our creativity to flourish. It nudges us toward balance—not by overwhelming us with efficiency but by gently encouraging a better harmony between our responsibilities and our passions. It's less about squeezing more into the hours of the day and more about shaping those hours to be more meaningful.

This partnership between humans and technology doesn't strive to replace our instincts or ingenuity; instead, it amplifies them. It reminds us that while the world around us grows more complex, the solutions we build can help bring clarity. These systems, when designed thoughtfully, inspire confidence rather than dependence, empowering us to navigate challenges with a sense of assurance and calm.

As we step further into this era of interconnected possibilities, the role of AI evolves from that of a servant to a companion. It walks beside us, not as an entity in command, but as a quiet force helping us to live with greater intention. By shaping our days to reflect what truly matters, these tools reaffirm a simple but profound truth: the greatest value of innovation lies not in the technology itself but in how it enhances our humanity.

Decision-Making in a Data-Driven World

Decision-making has always been a cornerstone of human experience. Every choice we make, from the smallest daily decisions to the most significant life-changing ones, shapes the course of our existence. But in a world increasingly driven by data, the way we approach decision-making is undergoing a profound transformation. What once relied heavily on intuition and experience is now being guided and informed by an unprecedented wealth of information, all brought to life by the power of artificial intelligence.

In this evolving landscape, data is no longer just a static resource—it's a dynamic force, capable of revealing patterns, insights, and possibilities that would otherwise remain hidden. Yet, as powerful as these tools are, their value lies not in replacing human judgment but in complementing it. At its best, a data-driven approach enhances our ability to think critically, act thoughtfully, and navigate uncertainty with greater confidence.

The beauty of data-driven decision-making is its ability to give us perspective. It takes the guesswork out of situations that once seemed unpredictable, offering clarity where there was confusion. Imagine a small business owner trying to decide how best to grow their company. By analyzing trends in customer behavior, buying patterns, and market demands, they can make choices rooted in evidence rather than assumption. Data doesn't just guide them; it empowers them to see the bigger picture while focusing on the details that matter most.

However, the human element in decision-making cannot and should not be ignored. Data, as sophisticated as it may be, is only as effective as the questions we ask of it. It's our curiosity, creativity, and values that shape the insights we seek. Numbers can tell us what is happening, but it's up to us to interpret why it matters and how to act on it. In this sense, the true power of data-driven decisions lies in the harmony between information and intuition—balancing what we know with what we feel.

This interplay becomes even more critical in moments where data alone cannot account for the complexities of human experience. No algorithm can fully grasp the emotional weight of a decision, or the ripple effects it might have on relationships, communities, or personal well-being. It's here that humanity becomes indispensable. Compassion, empathy, and a sense of purpose are what transform decisions from purely logical outcomes into meaningful actions.

Living in a data-driven world also means grappling with the responsibility that comes with access to so much information. The ethical implications of our choices grow more significant when data influences them. How do we ensure that the decisions we make are fair, just, and inclusive? How do we avoid being overwhelmed by information or falling into the trap of relying on it too heavily, forgetting the importance of human connection and context? These are challenges we must navigate thoughtfully, ensuring that data serves us, not the other way around.

Ultimately, decision-making in a data-driven world is not about perfection; it's about empowerment. It's about using the tools at our disposal to make choices that align with our values and aspirations. It's about embracing both the precision of data and the unpredictability of life, recognizing that every decision is an opportunity to learn, grow, and create something meaningful.

In this new era, we are reminded that while data can guide us, it's our humanity that defines us. The numbers may inform the journey, but it's our wisdom, compassion, and courage that chart the course. Together, these elements create a world where decisions are not just smarter but also richer, more thoughtful, and deeply connected to the essence of who we are.

Balancing data and intuition while data provides clarity and precision, it's crucial to acknowledge the role of human intuition in decision-making. Numbers and patterns can only take us so far; they describe what has happened or what might occur under certain conditions, but they don't account for the intangible factors that make each situation unique. Our instincts, honed by experience, allow us to interpret data within the context of our goals, values, and emotions.

For instance, a teacher analyzing test scores may use data to identify areas where students are struggling. However, their understanding of a student's personal challenges—things that no algorithm can capture—shapes how they approach solutions. In this way, intuition complements data, turning raw information into meaningful actions that resonate on a human level.

The danger of data overload in a world overflowing with information, the biggest challenge isn't accessing data—it's knowing how to use it effectively. Too much data can lead to paralysis, where decision-makers become so overwhelmed by options and possibilities that they struggle to act. This phenomenon, often called "analysis paralysis," highlights the need for discernment in a data-driven world.

To counteract this, it's essential to focus on relevance. The most effective decisions come from identifying the data that truly matters and filtering out the noise. This requires critical thinking and a clear understanding of goals. By simplifying the process and prioritizing actionable insights, we can transform overwhelming datasets into powerful tools for progress.

Ethics in data-driven decisions as data becomes a cornerstone of decision-making, ethical considerations take center stage. How we collect, interpret, and use data reflects our values as individuals and societies. Questions around privacy, bias, and fairness must be addressed to ensure that data-driven decisions are just and fair.

For example, AI systems used in hiring decisions might inadvertently favor certain demographics over others if the data they're trained on contains historical biases. It's the responsibility of those leveraging these tools to critically evaluate their systems, ensuring that decisions reflect ethical principles and don't perpetuate inequalities.

Transparency also plays a key role here. When data informs decisions, those affected should understand how and why choices are made. This openness fosters trust and accountability, bridging the gap between technology and the people it serves.

Empowering people through data at its best, data-driven decision-making is not about replacing human agency but enhancing it. The power of data lies in its ability to inform and empower individuals to make better choices, whether they're navigating personal goals, business strategies, or community planning. When wielded responsibly, data becomes a tool for empowerment, offering insights that enable people to act with greater clarity and confidence.

Imagine a farmer using weather and soil data to refine crop yields, or a family analyzing budget patterns to save for a dream vacation. These decisions, rooted in data, allow individuals to take control of their futures in meaningful ways. The real impact of data isn't in the numbers themselves—it's in how those numbers help people shape their lives.

The human touch in a data-driven world as data continues to shape decision-making, the need for human qualities like empathy, creativity, and judgment becomes even more critical. Decisions aren't just about efficiency or outcomes; they're about people and the lives affected by those choices. A hospital administrator deciding how to distribute resources based on patient data must also consider the emotional and psychological needs of the community they serve.

The most impactful decisions arise when data and humanity work together. Data provides the map, but humanity charts the course, ensuring that every decision reflects compassion, fairness, and purpose.

In a data-driven world, decision-making isn't just a skill—it's an art. It's about blending the precision of information with the depth of human understanding to create choices that are not only smart but also meaningful. By recognizing the strengths and limitations of data, embracing intuition, and prioritizing ethics, we can navigate this complex landscape with wisdom and purpose, shaping a future where technology amplifies our humanity rather than diminishes it.

To utterly understand the transformative power of data-driven decision-making, it's helpful to explore examples that demonstrate how this approach shapes industries, communities, and individual lives. Across various fields, the thoughtful use of data enables people to solve problems, seize opportunities, and create meaningful change—all while keeping a human-centered approach.

City planners face the challenge of creating spaces that accommodate growing populations while ensuring sustainability and livability. Data plays a critical role in these efforts. By analyzing patterns of movement, energy use, and resource consumption, planners can make informed decisions about where to build infrastructure, how to manage transportation systems, and how to reduce environmental impact.

For instance, a city might use traffic data collected from sensors on roads to show areas where congestion is consistently high. Instead of simply adding more lanes, which can lead to long-term inefficiencies, the city could use this data to redesign intersections, improve public transportation routes, or implement carpooling incentives. These changes reflect a human-first approach: solving logistical challenges while prioritizing the well-being of residents.

These are examples of data usage to improve life processes.

Healthcare: personalized patient care: in healthcare, data-driven decision-making is revolutionizing how treatments are planned and delivered. Imagine a rural clinic using data from patient records to show trends in local health issues, such as high rates of diabetes or respiratory conditions. By understanding these patterns, healthcare providers can distribute resources to address the most pressing concerns, such as organizing free diabetes screenings or increasing air quality awareness programs.

On an individual level, wearable devices that check heart rates, blood pressure, or activity levels generate real-time data that can guide both patients and doctors in making healthier choices. A doctor, for example, might notice that a patient's heart rate consistently spikes at specific times of the day, prompting a conversation about stress management or lifestyle changes. The key is that this data isn't just numbers—it's a story about the person's life, offering opportunities to intervene meaningfully.

Education: Shaping Student Success: This is another area where data-driven decision-making is reshaping the landscape. Teachers and administrators can use data to name patterns in student performance, attendance, and engagement. Rather than applying one-size-fits-all solutions, they can tailor interventions to meet the unique needs of each student.

For example, a school might notice through data analysis that certain students are struggling with math during specific times of the day. This insight could lead to restructuring the schedule so that math classes are held earlier when students are more alert. Similarly, tracking attendance data might reveal those students in certain neighborhoods face transportation challenges, prompting the introduction of a community bus program.

The focus here is not just on improving numbers—it's about ensuring every student has the opportunity to succeed in an environment that recognizes their individuality.

Small Businesses: Growth with Purpose

For small businesses, data-driven decision-making levels the playing field, allowing them to compete with larger enterprises by making smarter, more strategic choices. A local café, for instance, could analyze sales patterns to figure out which products are most popular during contrasting times of the day. If the data shows that breakfast items sell best during the week, but demand drops on weekends, the café might adjust its menu or hours to better align with customer behavior.

Beyond sales, small businesses can also use data to connect with their communities. For example, analyzing customer feedback—both online and in-person—can reveal what people value most about their experience. Whether it's a focus on sustainability, friendly service, or unique offerings, this information helps businesses stay true to their values while adapting to customer needs.

Agriculture: Feeding the Future

Farmers are increasingly turning to data to perfect yields and address global food security challenges. By collecting information on weather patterns, soil health, and crop performance, farmers can make more informed decisions about planting, irrigation, and harvesting. This isn't about industrial-scale operations; even small-scale farmers benefit from these insights.

Imagine a farmer using data to decide which crops are most resilient to changing climate conditions. With this knowledge, they can diversify their planting strategies, ensuring both economic stability and environmental sustainability. Data in this context becomes a tool not just for productivity but for resilience—helping farmers adapt to challenges while preserving their way of life.

Individual Decisions: Empowering Everyday Lives

Even at a personal level, data-driven decision-making is helping people navigate their daily lives with more intention. A family planning their monthly budget might track expenses using simple apps that categorize spending. By finding areas where they tend to overspend—such as dining out—they can make adjustments that align with their financial goals. Similarly, someone training for a marathon might use data from a fitness tracker to check progress, naming trends in performance and recovery. This enables them to adjust their training plan in a way that perfects results while minimizing the risk of injury.

These examples illustrate how data isn't just about efficiency—it's about empowerment. It gives individuals the tools to make decisions that reflect their priorities and aspirations, enhancing their quality of life in tangible ways.

Human-centered data use: at its core, data-driven decision-making isn't just about optimizing systems or increasing profits—it's about using information to serve people better. Whether it's improving a city's quality of life, addressing health disparities, or helping a small business thrive, the true power of data lies in its ability to enhance humanity.

However, the responsibility to use data ethically and thoughtfully stays paramount. It's not enough to rely on numbers; we must always ask how these decisions will impact real lives. By keeping people at the center of every data-driven choice, we can create a world where progress isn't just measured in metrics but felt in the well-being of individuals and communities alike.

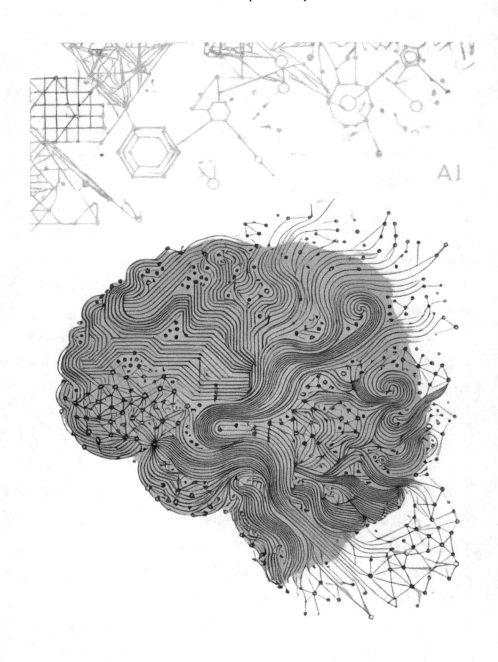

4 CHAPTER

ENTERTAINMENT REDEFINED: AI AS A CREATIVE FORCE

Insert Entertainment has always been a cornerstone of human culture, reflecting our stories, emotions, and imagination. Over the centuries, it has grown alongside technological advances, evolving from oral traditions to printed works, from silent films to immersive streaming experiences. With the advent of artificial intelligence, this landscape is undergoing a profound transformation. AI is no longer merely a tool for production; it has become a collaborator, reshaping how content is conceived, crafted, and experienced.

At its heart, storytelling has always been a deeply human endeavor. We create narratives to explore emotions, share experiences, and connect with others. Today, AI is stepping into the role of co-creator, offering new ways to break through creative blocks and push the boundaries of imagination. Writers, for instance, can rely on AI systems to suggest plot twists, develop nuanced characters, or propose thematic layers for their work. A filmmaker drafting a science fiction screenplay could describe a dystopian world and a resilient protagonist, and AI might propose unexpected plot elements that elevate the narrative. This collaboration accelerates the creative process without diminishing the distinctly human touch at the core of storytelling.

Music, long considered a universal language, is also undergoing a renaissance with AI. Composers and musicians are exploring uncharted territories, blending intuition with algorithmic innovation. AI systems, trained on vast libraries of compositions, can craft melodies that feel both familiar and novel. A musician may begin with a raw idea, layering harmonies or rhythms suggested by AI, resulting in pieces that defy traditional boundaries. The constructive collaboration between human creativity and machine-generated innovation expands the possibilities of what music can evoke. Even live performances are evolving, as AI-driven systems adapt music in real time to audience reactions, creating a shared experience that feels deeply personal.

Visual arts have embraced AI in ways that challenge traditional notions of authorship. Generative systems analyze artistic styles and reinterpret them into something entirely unique. Painters and digital artists experiment with AI to generate abstract designs, blending these creations with their own techniques. Beyond individual works, AI enables immersive environments that respond dynamically to viewers, transforming audiences from passive observers into active participants. The relationship between artist and technology becomes a dialogue, where each inspires the other.

Gaming is perhaps one of the most dynamic examples of AI's potential in entertainment. Worlds feel alive as characters and environments adapt to the choices players make. Non-player characters no longer follow predictable scripts but react with complexity, making each interaction feel genuine. Procedurally generated landscapes unfold organically, offering players an ever-changing canvas for exploration. Beyond traditional gaming, AI enhances educational and therapeutic experiences, tailoring content to personal learning styles or emotional states, further cementing gaming as a transformative medium.

Film and television production have embraced AI at every stage of the process. Casting decisions are guided by sophisticated systems that align talent with roles in ways that resonate with audiences. During production, AI streamlines editing, organizes scenes, and enhances visual effects. In post-production, these technologies refine details, ensuring seamless sound, color, and special effects. Beyond traditional formats, interactive films now let viewers shape narratives in real time, creating personalized cinematic experiences that redefine storytelling itself.

Perhaps one of the most impactful transformations brought by AI is the deeply personalized entertainment experience it enables. Streaming platforms curate content in ways that feel tailored to individual tastes. But this personalization goes further—imagine a service that crafts custom trailers based on someone's favorite genres or adjusts pacing and tone to match their preferences. Creators can offer alternative endings or perspectives, allowing audiences to engage with stories in ways that resonate most deeply.

This newfound creativity and accessibility also come with challenges. As AI becomes more integral to the entertainment process, questions arise about authenticity and ethics. Who owns a piece of AI-generated art? How do we ensure these creations respect the integrity of human artistry? These discussions are essential as we navigate the blending of human creativity with technological innovation.

Despite these questions, one thing is still clear: AI is not here to replace artists, musicians, or storytellers. It exists to amplify their vision, offering new tools to express the complexities of human experience. At its best, this partnership leads to creations that move us, connect us, and expand our understanding of what is possible. Entertainment, as it always has, stays a mirror to our collective imagination, now enhanced by the limitless potential of artificial intelligence.

Streaming Services and Personalized Content

In the digital age, streaming services have transformed into titans of entertainment, revolutionizing the way audiences experience and interact with content. Central to this evolution is the use of artificial intelligence, which allows platforms to deliver deeply personalized and immersive experiences. Unlike the era of traditional broadcasting, where content was curated for mass appeal, modern streaming services thrive on tailoring their offerings to individual preferences, fostering a uniquely intimate bond between viewer and platform.

AI's impact on streaming transcends the simplicity of recommendations. Today's sophisticated algorithms go beyond basic metrics, delving into viewing patterns, content engagement, and even the emotional nuances of the shows and movies we watch. This approach, known as "predictive personalization," redefines entertainment as an active dialogue between the viewer and the service. Imagine a platform seeing that a user enjoys slow-paced psychological thrillers and pairing that with supplementary content like director's commentaries, behind-the-scenes features, or discussions about the genre. This layered experience allows users to explore content more deeply, fostering a richer connection to the stories they consume.

More significantly, AI is beginning to influence the creative process itself. By analyzing massive datasets on audience behavior and preferences, streaming platforms can uncover trends and show gaps in their libraries. These insights inform the development of original programming, ensuring that new shows and films resonate with the ever-changing desires of their audience. For example, if data reveals a rising interest in stories about environmental challenges, platforms might greenlight eco-themed dramas or documentaries. This dynamic interaction between creators and audiences creates a feedback loop that pushes the boundaries of creative experimentation while staying deeply relevant to viewers.

Personalization doesn't stop at content recommendations. Streaming platforms are now exploring dynamic features that adapt to individual needs and lifestyles. Picture a scenario where a platform offers an abridged version of a feature-length film, perfect for someone seeking entertainment during a short break. Alternatively, imagine a service that adjusts a film's pacing or tone to suit a user's current mood, such as suggesting a light-hearted comedy after a streak of intense dramas. These innovations reshape entertainment into a flexible and adaptive companion, seamlessly integrating into the rhythms of everyday life. Features like tailored playlists, scene-specific recommendations, or interactive content further enrich the experience, making every moment spent with the platform feel deliberate and meaningful.

Yet, this surge in personalization raises pressing concerns. While AI-driven systems strive to align content with user preferences, there is a risk of narrowing horizons by over-catering to familiar tastes. These so-called "echo chambers" can limit exposure to diverse perspectives and ideas. To mitigate this, some platforms are designing algorithms that introduce calculated serendipity—offering content slightly outside a user's usual interests to encourage discovery and broaden their cultural repertoire. This balance between personalization and exploration is crucial in ensuring that entertainment is still a gateway to both comfort and growth.

Equally important are the ethical implications of data usage in streaming personalization. Many users are unaware of the depth and extent of data collected to enhance their experience. Transparency about how this data is gathered, analyzed, and applied is essential in fostering trust. Moreover, safeguarding user privacy while supporting the benefits of personalization requires a delicate balance, particularly as AI systems become increasingly sophisticated. Ethical considerations must be baked into these technologies to ensure they empower audiences without compromising their autonomy.

The integration of AI into streaming services has also sparked creative innovations in content production. With real-time data analysis, platforms can find which elements of a show or film resonate most with viewers, allowing creators to refine their work even after release. For instance, if audiences respond positively to a particular subplot or character, that feedback could shape future seasons or spin-offs. AI-enabled audience analytics offers creators invaluable insights into what moves and engages their viewers, enriching the storytelling process while keeping artistic integrity.

Furthermore, interactive content is benefiting immensely from AI personalization. Choose-your-own-adventure narratives are evolving into sophisticated, adaptive experiences where a user's choices influence not only the storyline but also the tone and pacing of the content. Imagine watching an interactive thriller where your decisions subtly alter the emotional weight of the plot, making the experience feel uniquely your own. Such innovations blur the line between creator and audience, transforming viewers into active participants in the storytelling process.

Another remarkable development is the role of AI in enhancing accessibility within streaming services. Features like auto-generated subtitles, audio descriptions, and customizable viewing options make content more inclusive for audiences with diverse needs. By analyzing user preferences and accessibility requirements, AI ensures that entertainment is not only personalized but also universally enjoyable. A platform might remember a user's preference for high-contrast subtitles or descriptive audio tracks, ensuring every interaction feels effortless and inclusive.

The evolution of streaming platforms driven by AI is also fostering global cultural exchange. By analyzing regional preferences and trends, platforms are increasingly commissioning content from diverse cultures and languages, introducing audiences to stories they might never have met otherwise. This globalization of entertainment broadens horizons and builds bridges between communities, proving that personalization can coexist with cultural discovery.

Soon, we could see the rise of entirely new companies within the streaming sector, specifically designed to cater to niche markets or hyper-personalized experiences. Imagine platforms that specialize in creating AI-generated content tailored to individual subscribers, where users could input themes, settings, or even specific character archetypes to generate custom films or series on demand. Alternatively, businesses could appear that function as intermediaries between creators and streaming platforms, using AI to match independent filmmakers with audiences most likely to appreciate their work. These companies would not only enrich the entertainment ecosystem but also empower creators and viewers to take control of their storytelling experiences.

Ultimately, AI-powered personalization is reshaping the very nature of streaming entertainment. By aligning content with the unique tastes and lifestyles of each viewer, these platforms craft experiences that feel deeply personal yet widely accessible. However, the success of this transformation hinges on the thoughtful integration of technology and creativity, ensuring that personalization enhances, rather than limits, the viewer's experience. As streaming services continue to evolve, their ability to balance innovation with ethics, individuality with diversity, and technology with humanity will define the future of entertainment.

The Evolution of Creativity in the Age of Machines

Creativity has always been considered a uniquely human trait, the spark that drives art, innovation, and storytelling. Yet, with the rise of artificial intelligence, the very definition of creativity is being reexamined. Machines, once relegated to executing predefined tasks, are now contributing to creative processes in ways that challenge our understanding of originality, collaboration, and authorship. This evolution is not merely technological but philosophical, reshaping how we view the act of creation itself.

Artificial intelligence is expanding the boundaries of creativity by functioning as both a collaborator and an independent creator. Algorithms can now analyze vast datasets, learning patterns, styles, and structures to produce works that rival those of human artists. For example, generative adversarial networks (GANs) can create visual art that mimics the styles of heads like Van Gogh or Picasso, while also generating entirely novel aesthetics. These creations raise questions: Is the machine imitating, or is it creating? Is the output an extension of the programmer's intent, or does the system have its own form of agency?

The concept of collaboration between humans and machines lies at the heart of this transformation. Artists, writers, and musicians increasingly use AI as a tool to enhance their processes. A musician might input a melody into an AI system, which then generates harmonies or alternative compositions. The artist's role shifts from sole creator to a kind of curator, selecting, refining, and blending the machine's contributions with their own vision. This symbiotic relationship pushes the boundaries of what is possible, enabling creators to explore uncharted territories of expression.

Narratives, too, are undergoing a profound shift. AI-powered systems can now analyze the structure of thousands of novels, showing recurring themes, character archetypes, and plot devices. Writers use these insights to craft stories that resonate more deeply with audiences or experiment with unconventional storytelling methods. Imagine a writer collaborating with an AI to develop a science fiction novel. The human author provides the emotional core and thematic direction, while the AI suggests plot twists, settings, and even dialogue. Together, they create a story that neither could have conceived alone.

Beyond collaboration, AI is venturing into the realm of autonomous creativity. Systems like OpenAI's GPT models have proved the ability to generate poetry, essays, and even screenplays that, in some cases, are indistinguishable from human-authored works. These outputs often blend logical coherence with surprising originality, sparking debate about whether machines are truly creative or merely simulating the process.

Ramón López de Mantras, in his exploration of artificial intelligence, emphasizes that creativity requires not just the ability to combine ideas but also a sense of purpose and intentionality—qualities machines still lack.

However, this evolution of creativity is not without challenges. One of the most pressing concerns is the question of authorship. If an AI-generated painting sells for millions, who owns the credit and the profit—the programmer, the user, or the machine? Legal frameworks are struggling to keep pace with these developments, highlighting the need for new paradigms that account for machine contributions to creative works.

Another challenge lies in the cultural implications of machine creativity. Will the proliferation of AI-generated content dilute the value we place on human-made art? Or will it lead to a renaissance of creativity, where human and machine efforts complement and elevate each other? Some fear that an overreliance on AI could stifle originality, as algorithms often draw from existing works rather than inventing entirely new forms. Others argue that the partnership between humans and machines will inspire creators to take greater risks, knowing they have tools to refine and support their ideas.

The evolution of creativity in the age of machines also has profound implications for education and skill development. As AI tools become more accessible, the barriers to entry for creative pursuits are lowered. An aspiring filmmaker with limited resources can use AI to generate storyboards, edit footage, or even compose a musical score. Similarly, students learning to write or paint can receive real-time feedback from

AI systems, accelerating their growth and expanding their horizons. These developments democratize creativity, allowing more people to take part in artistic and innovative endeavors.

Looking ahead, the role of AI in creativity will likely continue to evolve. Imagine a future where AI systems are not just tools but full-fledged collaborators, capable of understanding human emotions and cultural contexts. Such systems could contribute to projects that are not only technically impressive but also deeply meaningful. For instance, an AI might co-create a film that explores themes of identity and belonging, drawing on its ability to analyze and synthesize diverse cultural perspectives. In this vision, the distinction between human and machine creativity becomes less important than the impact of the work itself.

The interplay between humans and machines in the creative process highlights the ever-expanding possibilities of innovation. While machines bring computational power, speed, and pattern recognition to the table, humans contribute intuition, empathy, and the capacity for abstraction. Together, they form a partnership that pushes the boundaries of what art and innovation can achieve.

Ultimately, the evolution of creativity in the age of machines is not a story of replacement but of transformation. AI challenges us to rethink what it means to create, inspiring new methods, mediums, and modes of expression. As we navigate this uncharted territory, one thing is still clear: creativity, whether human, machine, or a combination of both, will continue to be a driving force in shaping our culture, our technology, and our understanding of the world.

How companies like Facebook are shaping creative content in the digital age in the ever-evolving landscape of the digital world, creativity is no longer confined to traditional mediums such as canvas, print, or cinema. Instead, it has found a dynamic playground in the virtual realm, where platforms like Facebook are transforming the way creative content is developed, shared, and consumed. With billions of users across the globe, Facebook has become a nexus of creativity, leveraging artificial intelligence and data-driven strategies to revolutionize content creation and user engagement.

Facebook's commitment to enhancing the creative potential of its platform lies in its robust use of artificial intelligence. The company utilizes AI to analyze user behavior, preferences, and interactions, crafting a personalized content experience that caters to diverse audiences. Through AI-driven algorithms, Facebook can suggest creative tools, recommend content improvements, and even automate parts of the creative process for users.

For instance, Facebook's AI-powered tools allow businesses and creators to design visually appealing posts, advertisements, and videos without requiring advanced design skills. Features like auto-generated layouts, font suggestions, and color matching provide creators with a toolkit that simplifies the creative process while maintaining professional quality. This democratization of design enables small businesses and independent creators to compete with larger brands, fostering a more inclusive creative ecosystem.

Boosting Engagement Through Data Insights

One of Facebook's strengths lies in its ability to harness user data to optimize content performance. By analyzing metrics such as click-through rates, likes, shares, and comments, the platform provides creators with actionable insights to refine their content. These data-driven recommendations help creators understand what resonates with their audience, enabling them to craft more engaging posts, videos, and campaigns.

For example, a small business owner promoting a product on Facebook might receive suggestions on the best times to post, the ideal length of a video, or the type of content—be it a carousel ad, a story, or a live broadcast—that aligns with audience preferences. This iterative approach to content creation allows creators to continuously improve, ensuring that their output remains fresh and relevant.

AI-Powered Content Moderation and Quality Control

In addition to fostering creativity, Facebook employs AI to maintain the quality and integrity of the content shared on its platform. Automated moderation systems review posts to ensure they meet community standards, removing harmful or inappropriate material. This focus on quality control not only protects users but also creates a safer and more inspiring environment for creators.

Beyond moderation, Facebook's AI systems also suggest enhancements to existing content. For instance, a user posting a photo might receive recommendations to apply filters, adjust lighting, or add text overlays to make the image more engaging. These small yet impactful suggestions help elevate the aesthetic and communicative value of creative posts.

Investing in Creator-Focused Initiatives

Recognizing the importance of creators in driving engagement, Facebook has launched several initiatives to support and empower creative individuals and businesses. Programs like Facebook's Creator Studio provide a centralized platform for managing content, tracking performance, and monetizing creative efforts. Features such as royalty-free music libraries and video editing tools give creators the resources they need to produce high-quality content efficiently.

Facebook is also investing in augmented reality (AR) and virtual reality (VR) technologies to expand the boundaries of creativity. Tools like Spark AR Studio enable creators to design interactive and immersive experiences, such as custom filters and effects for Instagram and Facebook Stories. These innovations encourage creators to experiment with new formats, enriching the digital content landscape with imaginative and interactive elements.

Nurturing community and collaboration: another key aspect of Facebook's approach to enhancing creative content is fostering a sense of community and collaboration. The platform's groups, pages, and events serve as hubs where creators can share ideas, seek feedback, and collaborate on projects. By connecting like-minded individuals,

Facebook facilitates the exchange of knowledge and inspiration, amplifying the collective creative potential of its user base.

For example, an independent filmmaker might join a Facebook group dedicated to short films, where they can share their work, receive constructive criticism, and collaborate with other creators on future projects. This sense of community not only supports individual growth but also contributes to the diversity and richness of content available on the platform.

The Future of Creativity on Facebook: Looking ahead, Facebook's role in shaping creative content is poised to grow even further. Advances in AI, AR, and VR will continue to expand the possibilities for creators, enabling them to produce content that is more engaging, interactive, and immersive. The integration of machine learning with user-generated content will also allow for greater personalization, ensuring that each user's experience feels uniquely tailored to their tastes and interests.

Additionally, Facebook's focus on accessibility and inclusivity will play a crucial role in democratizing creativity. By providing intuitive tools, actionable insights, and supportive communities, the platform ensures that anyone—regardless of their technical expertise or resources—can participate in the creative economy.

5 CHAPTER

THE WORKPLACE REVOLUTION: AI AS A PARTNER, NOT A REPLACEMENT

In an era of rapid technological advancement, artificial intelligence is reshaping the workplace in profound and unexpected ways. While early discussions often centered on fears of job displacement, a more nuanced perspective has emerged: ai as a collaborative partner rather than a replacement for human workers. By augmenting human abilities and streamlining processes, artificial intelligence is transforming how we work, fostering innovation, and redefining what it means to be productive.

Ai is no longer just a tool that automates repetitive tasks; it has evolved into an essential collaborator that enhances decision-making, creativity, and efficiency. Across industries ranging from healthcare to finance, ai systems analyze complex data, uncover patterns, and offer actionable insights that empower professionals to make informed decisions. In healthcare, for example, ai-powered diagnostic tools support doctors by detecting anomalies in medical imaging, allowing for faster and more accurate diagnoses. Similarly, in financial services, predictive analytics helps professionals anticipate market trends, reduce risks, and develop more robust strategies. These contributions underline the collaborative nature of ai, which excels at processing information while humans bring intuition, empathy, and context to the table. Together, they form a partnership that achieves results neither could attain independently.

One of ai's most transformative impacts on the workplace is its ability to optimize workflows. By automating routine tasks, it allows employees to focus on activities that require critical thinking and creativity. Human resources departments, for instance, benefit from ai-driven platforms that oversee the initial stages of recruitment, such as reviewing resumes and conducting preliminary assessments. This streamlining frees hr. professionals to devote more energy to strategic initiatives like fostering employee engagement and shaping organizational culture. In manufacturing, ai-powered robots enhance production lines by performing tasks that demand precision and consistency. Rather than replacing human workers, these robots complement their roles by taking on physically demanding or hazardous jobs, thereby improving safety and productivity. Similarly, customer service operations rely on ai chatbots to oversee basic inquiries, leaving human representatives to resolve more complex issues that require empathy and nuanced communication.

Ai's role in enhancing workplace creativity is equally significant and often overlooked. By generating design concepts, proposing innovative solutions, or analyzing consumer trends, ai acts as a catalyst for creativity across diverse fields. In marketing, for example, ai tools provide insights into consumer behavior and emerging trends, enabling campaigns that resonate with specific audiences. Graphic designers and content creators benefit from ai-powered software that facilitates experimentation with new styles, accelerates production timelines, and refines the quality of their work. Beyond artistic and communicative domains, ai is fueling innovation in engineering and product development. Engineers use ai to simulate and evaluate designs, identifying potential flaws or improvements before creating physical prototypes. This not only saves time and resources but also encourages bold experimentation, with ai providing a safety net for ambitious projects.

The integration of ai into the workplace is also driving greater inclusivity and adaptability. Ai-powered tools like voice recognition software, real-time translation, and adaptive interfaces empower employees with diverse needs to contribute fully. Hearing-impaired professionals, for instance, can participate in meetings through ai-driven transcription services, while visually impaired employees use ai tools to navigate digital workspaces more effectively. Remote and hybrid work models have also benefited from ai, as advanced video conferencing platforms use ai to enhance audio clarity, provide real-time translations, and analyze meeting dynamics. These advancements ensure that teams remain connected and productive regardless of geographical barriers, creating a more accessible and equitable work environment.

As artificial intelligence becomes more deeply embedded in the workplace, ethical considerations must take precedence. Transparency about how ai systems function is essential for building trust among employees and stakeholders. Workers need clarity on how ai tools support decision-making, especially in sensitive areas like performance evaluations or hiring processes. Companies that prioritize transparency foster a culture of trust and collaboration, ensuring that employees view ai as an ally rather than a threat. Addressing biases in ai systems is another critical concern. Since these systems learn from historical data, they can unintentionally perpetuate existing inequalities if not carefully monitored. Organizations must invest in diverse datasets and implement continuous oversight to ensure fairness and equity in ai-driven processes.}

The rise of ai underscores the importance of lifelong learning and adaptability in the workforce. As roles evolve, employees must acquire new skills to thrive in an ai-enhanced environment. Organizations play a pivotal role by offering training programs that focus on technical expertise as well as soft skills such as emotional intelligence, problem-solving, and adaptability. A marketing professional, for instance, might learn to interpret insights from ai analytics tools, while a factory worker receives training to operate and maintain ai-powered machinery. These initiatives not only equip employees to remain competitive but also foster confidence and resilience in the face of technological change.

Ai's integration into the workplace is fundamentally altering traditional notions of work, productivity, and collaboration. It enables workers to focus on what they do best—thinking creatively, solving complex problems, and building meaningful connections—while overseeing repetitive or data-intensive tasks with unparalleled efficiency. This partnership between human ingenuity and machine capability fosters innovation, drives efficiency, and creates opportunities for growth that benefit both individuals and organizations.

Ultimately, the workplace revolution driven by ai is not about replacement but transformation. It challenges us to rethink roles, embrace new possibilities, and reimagine a future where technology amplifies human potential rather than diminishing it. The most successful workplaces will be those that harness ai's capabilities to enhance, rather than overshadow, the uniquely human qualities that define us. By fostering a culture of collaboration, trust, and adaptability, organizations can ensure that ai remains a powerful partner in building a more innovative, inclusive, and dynamic future for work.

Leveraging ai on private networks for secure and optimized business operations

In the evolving digital landscape, businesses in the private sector are increasingly adopting artificial intelligence to optimize operations, enhance decision-making, and foster innovation. However, with the growing reliance on ai comes a heightened need to ensure that sensitive information remains protected. For organizations that manage proprietary data, intellectual property, or strategic documents, utilizing controlled private networks, such as secure ethernet infrastructures, can offer a solution that aligns efficiency with security.

The integration of ai within private networks begins with creating an environment where ai tools operate exclusively within the confines of an organization's internal infrastructure. By isolating these systems from public internet access, companies can significantly reduce the risk of external threats, such as data breaches or unauthorized access. This approach not only safeguards sensitive information but also ensures that ai algorithms focus solely on analyzing and optimizing internal resources without external interference.

One of the primary advantages of employing ai within private networks is the capacity to control data flow meticulously. Organizations can configure these networks to limit access to specific departments or teams, ensuring that data is only accessible to those who require it for their roles. For example, a company's research and development team might utilize ai to refine prototypes, analyze market trends, or simulate product performance scenarios. By restricting ai operations to the private network, businesses ensure that these activities remain confidential and protected from external observation.

In addition to isolating ai systems, businesses can implement robust encryption protocols to further enhance security. Encryption ensures that even if data were intercepted, it would remain incomprehensible to unauthorized entities. This layered approach to securing ai processes creates a robust foundation for operational excellence without compromising the integrity of sensitive materials.

Another key element in leveraging ai within private networks is the implementation of stringent data governance policies. These policies define how data is collected, stored, and utilized within the organization. By establishing clear guidelines, businesses can ensure that ai applications align with ethical standards and legal requirements. For instance, companies can employ anonymization techniques to protect individual identities while still allowing ai to analyze aggregated data for insights. Such practices demonstrate a commitment to transparency and accountability, building trust among employees, partners, and stakeholders.

To prevent potential distractions and maintain productivity, organizations can adopt intelligent filtering systems within their private networks. These systems monitor and prioritize data traffic, ensuring that ai tools access only the information relevant to their designated tasks. This targeted approach minimizes inefficiencies and ensures that computational resources are directed toward activities that drive value for the organization. For example, a financial institution might employ ai to detect anomalies in transaction patterns, flagging potential risks or opportunities. By limiting the scope of ai to transactional data and excluding unrelated information, the institution maximizes the tool's effectiveness while preserving operational focus.

Establishing a culture of digital responsibility is equally vital in ensuring the effective integration of ai within private networks.

Employees must be educated about the importance of maintaining secure data practices and adhering to established protocols. Regular training sessions can empower teams to recognize potential vulnerabilities and take initiative-taking measures to mitigate risks. Furthermore, fostering open communication about the organization's ai initiatives helps employees understand the benefits and limitations of these technologies, promoting a sense of collaboration and shared purpose.

The adoption of ai within private networks also opens avenues for enhancing resource allocation and operational efficiency. For instance, ai-driven predictive analytics can optimize supply chain processes by forecasting demand, identifying bottlenecks, and suggesting inventory adjustments. Similarly, manufacturing firms can rely on ai to monitor equipment performance, detecting signs of wear or potential failures before they escalate into costly disruptions. By operating within secure private networks, these applications function without exposing critical operational data to external entities, ensuring that businesses retain control over their strategic assets.

To further optimize their ai-driven processes, companies can invest in advanced monitoring and auditing tools. These tools provide real-time insights into ai activities, allowing businesses to evaluate performance, identify areas for improvement, and ensure compliance with internal policies. For example, a technology firm using ai for software development might employ monitoring systems to track coding efficiency, error rates, and project timelines. By integrating these tools within a controlled network environment, the firm gains a comprehensive understanding of its operations without compromising security.

Collaboration with trusted technology partners is another essential aspect of implementing ai within private networks. Organizations should prioritize collaborating with providers who demonstrate a commitment to data security and transparency. Collaborative efforts can involve co-developing customized ai solutions that address specific business needs while adhering to stringent security standards. These partnerships enable companies to leverage external expertise without exposing sensitive information to unnecessary risks.

As organizations embrace ai to achieve operational excellence, they must also remain vigilant about evolving threats. Cybersecurity strategies must be dynamic, adapting to new challenges as they emerge. Regular assessments of network vulnerabilities, coupled with timely updates to security protocols, ensure that businesses stay ahead of potential risks. Additionally, engaging in industry forums or knowledge-sharing initiatives can help companies stay informed about emerging best practices and technological advancements.

The integration of ai within private networks represents a change in basic assumptions in how businesses approach innovation and efficiency. By creating secure, controlled environments where ai tools can thrive, organizations unlock the potential for transformative growth while safeguarding their most valuable assets. This approach underscores the importance of balancing technological advancement with responsibility, ensuring that progress is achieved without compromising the trust of employees, partners, and stakeholders. In this evolving landscape, businesses that embrace ai as a strategic partner within secure private networks position themselves for sustained success and resilience in an increasingly digital world.

Automation, efficiency, and the human touch

The intersection of automation and efficiency represents a pivotal evolution in how businesses function, driving both innovation and productivity. Yet, even in a landscape increasingly shaped by technological advancements, the human element remains irreplaceable. This delicate balance between automated systems and the nuanced judgment of human professionals is redefining modern workflows and establishing a new standard for success in the workplace.

Automation is revolutionizing industries by streamlining processes that were once time intensive. From manufacturing to healthcare, automated systems now perform repetitive, precise, and data-driven tasks with unparalleled consistency. Assembly lines, for instance, are benefiting from robotics that execute intricate operations without fatigue, enhancing output and reducing error rates. Similarly, in sectors such as coordination, automated sorting and routing systems ensure the timely delivery of goods, optimizing supply chain dynamics in ways that were previously unattainable.

However, automation is not merely about executing tasks faster; it also enhances decision-making by providing insights derived from complex datasets. In finance, algorithms analyze market trends, offering predictive models that guide investment strategies. In customer service, intelligent chat systems address routine inquiries while collecting valuable feedback, ensuring consistent interactions without overwhelming human teams. These systems exemplify how automation enables organizations to scale their operations while maintaining an elevated level of accuracy and responsiveness.

Despite these advancements, the role of human expertise remains crucial. Automated systems excel in pattern recognition and repetition but lack the capacity for intuition, empathy, and creative problem-solving. Human professionals bridge this gap, interpreting the outputs of automated tools and applying contextual understanding to ensure that outcomes align with broader objectives. For example, while an ai system might flag anomalies in financial transactions, a financial analyst's expertise is essential to discern whether these anomalies are legitimate risks or routine variations.

Moreover, the human element is indispensable in fostering trust and connection. In industries like healthcare, patients value the empathy and reassurance that only a human caregiver can provide. Automation might assist in diagnostics and treatment planning, but the patient experience is deeply enriched by the interpersonal interactions that build confidence and understanding. Similarly, in creative fields, technology serves as an enabler rather than a substitute, assisting designers, writers, and artists in realizing their visions while leaving the essence of creativity to human ingenuity.

A key to achieving harmony between automation and the human touch lies in the thoughtful integration of technology into workflows. This requires not only the adoption of advanced tools but also a commitment to continuous learning and adaptation. Organizations must empower their workforce with training that enhances their ability to collaborate with automated systems effectively. Professionals who understand how to interpret, refine, and build upon the outputs of these systems are better positioned to drive innovation and achieve strategic goals.

Ethical considerations also play a significant role in this integration. As automation becomes more pervasive, it is essential to address concerns about data privacy, transparency, and fairness. Systems must be designed to operate within ethical frameworks that respect individual rights and promote equitable outcomes. Involving diverse teams in the development and deployment of automated tools ensures that these systems are both inclusive and reflective of varied perspectives.

Furthermore, organizations must recognize the importance of cultivating a workplace culture that values both technological efficiency and human creativity. Encouraging collaboration, fostering open communication, and providing opportunities for professional growth ensure that employees feel valued and engaged in the face of technological change. By emphasizing the human contributions that cannot be replicated by machines, companies not only enhance their competitive advantage but also build resilient and adaptable teams.

As industries continue to evolve, the interplay between automation, efficiency, and the human touch will define the trajectory of progress. Businesses that embrace this balance—leveraging technology to enhance productivity while championing the irreplaceable qualities of human insight—position themselves at the forefront of innovation. In this new era, success is not measured solely by how efficiently tasks are completed but by how seamlessly technology and humanity come together to create value, solve problems, and inspire trust.

Expanding human optimization through ai-powered tools

The role of artificial intelligence in reshaping workplace dynamics has transitioned from experimental to indispensable, offering solutions that go beyond efficiency and delve into the realm of human optimization. Ai-powered tools are no longer confined to streamlining processes; they now empower individuals to maximize their potential, fostering environments where creativity, decision-making, and productivity are seamlessly enhanced.

Central to this evolution is the emergence of platforms designed to support professionals across diverse domains. These tools operate not as standalone technologies but as collaborative frameworks that integrate deeply with human workflows. For instance, **kissflow** provides comprehensive process automation while remaining adaptable to the nuanced needs of teams, ensuring that repetitive tasks are minimized, and mental energy is reserved for strategic thinking. Similarly, **workfusion** leverages intelligent automation to manage complex operational workflows, reducing bottlenecks and enabling teams to focus on higher-value contributions.

In the realm of personal productivity, ai-driven platforms such as **otter.ai** and **Grammarly** exemplify the shift toward tools that enhance cognitive capabilities. **Otter.ai**, for example, generates real-time transcriptions of meetings, complete with actionable highlights and searchable summaries, ensuring that important insights are not lost amid lengthy discussions. On the other hand, **Grammarly** refines written communication by offering advanced suggestions that go beyond grammar corrections, promoting clarity and tone alignment suited to diverse professional contexts.

Ai-powered tools also excel in fostering collaboration within teams. Platforms like **miro** and **figma** facilitate interactive design and brainstorming sessions, allowing multiple users to contribute simultaneously, regardless of their location. These systems encourage dynamic exchanges of ideas, breaking down traditional silos and enabling seamless innovation. By combining intuitive interfaces with advanced analytics, these tools ensure that creative processes remain fluid and inclusive.

In industries that demand precision and foresight, predictive analytics has become an invaluable asset. **Sisense**, for instance, transforms vast datasets into actionable intelligence, guiding decisions with visualized insights that are both accessible and comprehensive. For marketing teams, platforms such as **marketo engage** utilize machine learning to anticipate customer behaviors, enabling campaigns that resonate with specific audience segments and optimize engagement metrics. These tools not only provide clarity in strategy but also empower teams to adapt in real time to evolving trends.

For organizations focused on employee development, ai offers transformative solutions. **Betterup,** an ai-enhanced coaching platform, combines behavioral science with machine learning to deliver personalized growth strategies for employees at all levels. It identifies areas where individuals can improve, tailoring coaching sessions to align with both personal aspirations and organizational objectives. In learning and development, **edcast** serves as a knowledge-sharing hub, curating resources based on employee roles and career trajectories, ensuring that continuous learning becomes an integral part of professional growth.

The integration of artificial intelligence in organizational operations also extends to project management. Tools like **Smartsheet** and **clickup** incorporate ai functionalities that optimize task assignments, identify potential delays, and recommend adjustments to meet deadlines. By presenting managers with real-time insights into project progress, these platforms enhance accountability while fostering initiative-taking problem-solving.

However, the true value of ai-driven tools lies not just in their ability to optimize tasks but in their capacity to amplify human strengths. Tools like **crystal knows** utilize ai to analyze communication styles, helping professionals tailor their interactions to resonate more effectively with colleagues and clients. This human-centric approach ensures that technology enhances emotional intelligence and people skills, areas where machines serve as enablers rather than substitutes.

Security and ethical considerations remain paramount in the adoption of ai tools. Platforms such as **IBM's Watson openscale** provide transparency by monitoring ai decisions and identifying biases, ensuring fairness in automated processes. Similarly, **vanta** offers continuous compliance monitoring, safeguarding sensitive data and ensuring that organizations meet stringent regulatory standards. These systems underline the importance of accountability in ai integration, demonstrating that efficiency must not come at the cost of trust.

The continued development of ai-powered tools for human optimization represents a transformative shift in how organizations approach both productivity and innovation. By providing tailored support that complements human expertise, these platforms create environments where employees can thrive. This convergence of technology and humanity is not merely about enhancing workflows but about empowering individuals to unlock their full potential, fostering a future where progress is driven by collaboration between minds and machines.

Skills for the ai-driven workplace

The transformation brought about by artificial intelligence in professional environments demands a reevaluation of the skills required to thrive. As ai tools and systems redefine workflows, decision-making, and innovation, individuals must cultivate a set of competencies that complement and enhance these advancements. These skills are not solely technical; they extend into areas that emphasize adaptability, strategic thinking, and emotional intelligence, creating a workforce that can leverage technology without losing its human essence.

A foundational skill in the ai-driven workplace is digital fluency. This encompasses the ability to interact effectively with ai-powered tools and platforms, understanding their functionalities and limitations. Workers who grasp the mechanics of ai systems can interpret their outputs and use them to inform strategic decisions. For example, familiarity with platforms like tableau or power bi enables professionals to transform raw data into actionable insights, fostering a more informed approach to problem-solving.

Equally important is the ability to adapt to evolving technological landscapes. Ai systems are dynamic, with continuous updates and innovations shaping their capabilities. Professionals must embrace a mindset of lifelong learning, staying informed about emerging trends and tools. Platforms such as LinkedIn learning and Coursera offer tailored courses that equip individuals with up-to-date knowledge, ensuring they remain competitive in an ever-changing environment.

Critical thinking is another essential skill, as ai systems often provide recommendations based on historical data and algorithms. Human oversight is crucial to evaluate these outputs, contextualize them, and ensure they align with organizational objectives. For instance, an ai might suggest strategies based on predictive analytics, but it is the responsibility of the professional to assess whether those strategies are ethical, viable, and aligned with long-term goals. This ability to critically assess ai-generated insights ensures that decisions are both data-driven and contextually appropriate.

In addition to technical and analytical skills, emotional intelligence takes on heightened importance in the ai-enabled workplace. While machines excel at data processing, they lack the capacity for empathy, understanding, and relationship-building. Professionals who can navigate interpersonal dynamics, foster collaboration, and resolve conflicts bring an invaluable dimension to ai-integrated teams. Tools like crystal knows assist in enhancing communication by offering insights into colleagues' communication styles, but the ultimate responsibility for building trust and rapport remains with humans.

Strategic foresight is another critical competency. As ai transforms industries, professionals must anticipate shifts and proactively position themselves and their organizations for success. This involves not only understanding current capabilities of ai but also envisioning its future applications. For instance, supply chain managers who grasp how predictive analytics can optimize planning will be better prepared to adopt and implement ai solutions that enhance operational efficiency. Similarly, marketing leaders who anticipate consumer trends through platforms like marketo engage can craft campaigns that resonate with evolving customer preferences.

Moreover, the ability to bridge technical and non-technical domains is increasingly valuable. Professionals who can translate complex ai concepts into actionable insights for diverse audiences play a pivotal role in aligning technological innovations with business objectives. This requires persuasive communication skills coupled with an understanding of both the technical and strategic aspects of ai applications. For example, data scientists who can articulate the implications of their findings to executive teams enable more effective decision-making and cross-departmental collaboration.

Ethical awareness is also paramount in navigating the ai-driven workplace. Professionals must ensure that ai systems are deployed responsibly, avoiding biases and ensuring fairness in outcomes. Understanding the principles of ethical ai—including transparency, accountability, and inclusivity—is crucial for fostering trust in these technologies. Platforms like IBM's Watson openscale provide tools for monitoring and mitigating biases, but ethical vigilance ultimately depends on human oversight.

Teamwork and collaboration remain at the heart of professional success, even in ai-integrated environments. Ai can enhance team efficiency by streamlining communication and automating routine tasks, but the human ability to collaborate creatively and empathetically is irreplaceable. Tools like slack or Microsoft teams, which integrate ai functionalities to optimize workflows, demonstrate how technology supports teamwork without substituting the personal connections that drive innovation.

Resilience and adaptability round out the key skills for the ai-driven workplace. The pace of technological advancement requires professionals to embrace change with agility and a solutions-oriented mindset. Challenges posed by integrating ai systems or navigating disruptions demand a level of flexibility and determination that only human resilience can provide. Leaders who model adaptability inspire their teams to approach challenges as opportunities for growth and innovation.

The emergence of ai as a cornerstone of modern workplaces calls for an integrated approach to skill development. While technical competencies such as data analysis and digital fluency form the foundation, they must be complemented by critical thinking, emotional intelligence, and strategic foresight. Ethical awareness, communication skills, and resilience further ensure that individuals can navigate the complexities of ai integration effectively.

By cultivating these skills, professionals not only enhance their value in the workforce but also contribute to a balanced and human-centered approach to technological progress. The ai-driven workplace is not a space where machines replace people but a collaborative environment where technology amplifies human potential, enabling teams to achieve goals that were once thought unattainable.

6 CHAPTER

AI IN SOCIAL CONNECTIONS: ENHANCING RELATIONSHIPS OR CREATING DIVIDES?

The rise of artificial intelligence has not only reshaped industries and transformed workplaces but has also infiltrated the very fabric of human relationships. As technology becomes increasingly intertwined with how we connect, communicate, and foster relationships, questions emerge about its true impact. Does AI serve as a bridge, enhancing human connections, or does it subtly construct divides, isolating individuals behind screens and algorithms? This duality lies at the heart of our exploration.

At its best, AI offers tools that bring people together, transcending geographical and cultural barriers. Consider how language translation algorithms enable real-time communication between individuals who would otherwise be unable to converse. Applications like **Google Translate** or AI-enhanced live interpretation systems have allowed friendships, collaborations, and even romantic relationships to flourish across linguistic divides. Similarly, platforms like **Zoom** or **Microsoft Teams**, powered by AI-enhanced audio and video optimization, have become essential in maintaining personal and professional connections during times of physical separation.

Social media platforms provide another layer of connectivity, employing AI to curate content and suggest new connections. Algorithms analyze user behaviors, preferences, and interactions to recommend friends, groups, or content, creating a personalized social experience. For instance, AI-powered features on platforms like **Facebook** or **LinkedIn** enable individuals to reconnect with long-lost acquaintances or establish professional networks that align with their aspirations. These technologies amplify opportunities to interact, collaborate, and bond in ways that were unimaginable a few decades ago.

Yet, the same tools that unite us can also foster disconnection. One of the most significant concerns is the potential for algorithmic biases and echo chambers. AI-driven systems often prioritize content that aligns with a user's existing preferences, inadvertently reinforcing viewpoints and isolating individuals from diverse perspectives. On social platforms, this can lead to polarized communities where engagement is fueled by confrontation rather than understanding. The very algorithms designed to connect us may unintentionally create digital silos, narrowing our exposure to differing ideas and experiences.

Another point of contention is the authenticity of connections mediated by AI. Chatbots and virtual companions, such as **Replika** or AI-driven customer support agents, simulate human interaction with increasing sophistication. While these systems offer companionship and assistance, they raise ethical questions about the nature of relationships formed with entities devoid of consciousness. Can an interaction with a machine be considered a genuine connection, or does it erode the value of human empathy and presence? Such questions delve into the core of what it means to relate to another being.

The role of AI in dating and romantic relationships further underscores this complexity. Platforms like **Tinder** and **Bumble** employ AI to analyze user behavior, preferences, and even micro expressions to suggest potential matches. While this increases efficiency in finding compatible partners, it also reduces the spontaneity and serendipity traditionally associated with romance. Furthermore, the reliance on AI-generated compatibility scores risks commodifying relationships, shifting focus from genuine emotional connection to data-driven optimization.

Despite these challenges, AI's potential to enhance relationships cannot be overlooked. Consider its role in accessibility and inclusion. For individuals with disabilities, AI-powered tools such as voice-to-text applications, adaptive communication devices, or emotion-recognition systems facilitate meaningful interactions that might otherwise be hindered. These advancements not only empower individuals but also create opportunities for more inclusive communities where everyone can participate equally in social and professional spheres.

In educational and workplace settings, AI-driven platforms like **Slack** or **Edmodo** foster collaboration and teamwork by streamlining communication and providing personalized learning or task recommendations. These tools ensure that individuals can connect more effectively, bridging gaps in knowledge and fostering mutual growth. Additionally, AI's ability to analyze group dynamics and suggest strategies for conflict resolution enhances its role as a mediator, improving the quality of relationships in high-pressure environments.

Yet, as Clifford A. Pick over might argue, the role of technology in human evolution is as much about what we lose as what we gain. The increasing reliance on AI in personal interactions risks diminishing our capacity for deep, empathetic connection. The subtle cues of body language, tone, and presence—integral elements of human communication—are often lost in AI-mediated interactions. This reductionist approach to relationships may cultivate superficial bonds, where the richness of human experience is replaced by transactional exchanges.

To navigate these complexities, a balanced approach is essential. Policymakers, technologists, and users must work collaboratively to ensure that AI systems prioritize ethical considerations and foster genuine connection. Transparency in how algorithms operate, coupled with safeguards against biases and misuse, can mitigate many of the negative impacts associated with AI-driven social tools. Educational initiatives that promote digital literacy and emphasize the importance of authentic communication are equally critical in equipping individuals to use AI responsibly.

There are five key questions about social connections that we should consider fostering unity rather than divide opinions.

1. How does AI enhance personal relationships across geographical boundaries?

AI-powered tools have revolutionized global communication by breaking down language and accessibility barriers. Real-time translation services, such as those offered by **Google Translate** or **Microsoft Translator**, allow individuals from different linguistic backgrounds to engage in meaningful conversations without misunderstanding. Video conferencing platforms, enhanced with AI for noise reduction and language support, enable seamless interactions across time zones. These innovations foster connections that would have been improbable in a pre-AI era, enabling friendships, collaborations, and even romantic relationships to flourish despite physical distances.

2. Can AI replace genuine human connections in social settings?

AI cannot fully replicate the depth and authenticity of human connections. While virtual companions and chatbots, such as **Replika**, provide comfort and simulate empathy, they lack consciousness and the emotional complexity that defines human interactions. AI tools are valuable for addressing loneliness or supporting users with specific needs, but they fall short of replicating the nuances of a relationship built on shared experiences, trust, and genuine emotion. Rather than replacing human connections, AI is best positioned as a complementary tool to enhance or facilitate existing relationships.

3. What challenges do AI-driven algorithms pose in fostering unbiased social interactions?

AI algorithms, when designed without careful oversight, can inadvertently create echo chambers and reinforce biases. These systems often prioritize content or connections aligned with a user's existing preferences, limiting exposure to diverse perspectives. For instance, social media platforms may amplify polarized views to increase engagement, fostering divisions rather than dialogue. Addressing this requires transparency in algorithm design, diverse training datasets, and regular audits to ensure fairness and inclusivity in how AI fosters social connections.

4. How is AI being used to improve inclusivity in communication for individuals with disabilities?

AI has significantly improved inclusivity through tools that cater to diverse communication needs. For example, voice-to-text applications enable hearing-impaired individuals to participate in conversations seamlessly. AI-driven emotion recognition systems assist those with autism in interpreting social cues, while adaptive devices powered by machine learning help users with motor impairments communicate more effectively. These technologies not only facilitate participation in social and professional settings but also empower individuals to connect with others in ways that were previously inaccessible.

5. Does AI in social applications risk eroding the authenticity of human relationships?

There is a legitimate concern that AI's growing role in mediating relationships might diminish the authenticity of human interactions. Over-reliance on AI tools for communication or emotional support can lead to transactional relationships where meaningful connection is replaced by convenience. To mitigate this, it is essential to use AI as an enhancer rather than a substitute for genuine interaction. By fostering a balance—where technology supports but does not overshadow the human element—users can maintain the authenticity and richness of their relationships while benefiting from the efficiencies AI offers.

The question of whether AI enhances relationships or creates divides is not binary. Its impact lies in how we choose to integrate it into our lives. When designed and employed thoughtfully, AI has the potential to bridge distances, amplify inclusivity, and enrich human interactions. However, when misused or left unchecked, it risks eroding the essence of what makes relationships meaningful. As we stand at this intersection of innovation and connection, the challenge is not merely to embrace AI but to do so in a way that uplifts and preserves our shared humanity.

AI-Powered Social Media Algorithms: Understanding and Utilizing Them Effectively

Artificial intelligence has become the backbone of social media platforms, shaping the content we see, the connections we make, and the experiences we have online. AI-powered algorithms analyze vast amounts of user data to personalize feeds, recommend content, and enhance engagement. While these systems offer unparalleled convenience and efficiency, their influence is profound, requiring mindful usage to ensure they serve as tools for connection rather than division.

AI algorithms on platforms like Instagram, Facebook, and TikTok are designed to optimize user engagement. They do so by analyzing behaviors such as likes, shares, comments, and time spent on specific posts. These insights allow algorithms to prioritize content that aligns with individual preferences, creating a highly tailored experience. For example, someone who frequently interacts with travel-related posts will likely see more content about destinations, tips, or influencers in that domain.

However, this personalization comes with potential challenges. Echo chambers—digital spaces where users are primarily exposed to viewpoints like their own—can emerge, limiting diverse perspectives and reinforcing biases. Over time, this can hinder meaningful dialogue and reduce exposure to innovative ideas. Additionally, algorithms may prioritize sensational or emotionally charged content to maximize engagement, further complicating efforts to maintain balanced and constructive interactions.

To harness the benefits of AI-powered social media algorithms while mitigating their downsides, consider the following strategies:

1. **Diversify Your Interactions**: Engage with a broad range of content to signal the algorithm to offer varied recommendations. Actively seek out accounts or topics outside your usual

preferences to encourage exposure to different perspectives.

2. **Review Your Preferences Regularly**: Many platforms allow users to adjust their settings or preferences. Take time to review and update these settings to align with your evolving interests and priorities.

3. **Be Intentional with Engagement**: Interact thoughtfully with content rather than passively scrolling. Likes, shares, and comments all inform the algorithm, so use these actions to shape your feed toward what truly adds value to your experience.

4. **Utilize Platform Tools**: Explore features like "See Less" or "Hide Post" to fine-tune the content displayed. These tools provide immediate feedback to the algorithm about what aligns with your preferences.

5. **Monitor Time Spent**: Use time management tools available on many platforms to track your usage and set limits. Maintaining a balanced online presence helps mitigate overexposure to curated content and encourages offline connections.

6. **Engage with Credible Sources**: Prioritize interactions with content from reputable and diverse sources. This not only improves the quality of your feed but also helps counter misinformation often amplified by poorly monitored algorithms.

Understanding how AI-powered social media algorithms function empowers users to navigate these platforms more effectively. By actively shaping your digital environment, you can leverage these systems to enrich your online interactions, foster diverse connections, and promote meaningful engagement. With mindful use, these algorithms can evolve from simple engagement drivers to tools for personal and social growth.

For example: OpenAI's advanced language models, such as GPT, offer transformative capabilities that can be harnessed to design and refine social media algorithms. These tools excel in natural language processing, contextual understanding, and sentiment analysis, making them invaluable for platforms aiming to create more personalized and engaging user experiences. By integrating OpenAI-powered functionalities, developers and organizations can optimize content delivery, foster meaningful interactions, and address the challenges associated with traditional algorithms.

How OpenAI Supports Social Media Algorithm Development

1. **Content Recommendation Systems**: OpenAI models can analyze user behavior, preferences, and historical interactions to generate highly personalized content recommendations. By understanding the context of a user's interests, the algorithm can prioritize posts, articles, or media that align with their preferences while introducing diverse perspectives.

2. **Sentiment Analysis and Moderation**: OpenAI's natural language processing capabilities enable platforms to assess the sentiment of posts and comments. This allows for real-time moderation of harmful content, ensuring that platforms maintain a positive and respectful environment. For example, an OpenAI-powered system can flag abusive language or misinformation, reducing the risk of echo chambers and toxicity.

3. **Dynamic Content Creation**: Platforms can use OpenAI to auto-generate captions, descriptions, or promotional content tailored to user

engagement trends. This feature not only enhances the platform's appeal but also supports creators by automating repetitive tasks, freeing up their time for more strategic efforts.

4. **Enhanced Chatbots and Virtual Assistants**: OpenAI-powered chatbots provide advanced conversational capabilities, offering users an interactive and intuitive experience. These bots can oversee customer support queries, recommend relevant groups or content, and facilitate smoother interactions between users and the platform.

5. **Data-Driven Insights for Algorithm Training**: By processing vast datasets, OpenAI models can identify trends and anomalies, offering actionable insights for algorithm refinement. Developers can use this data to improve recommendation accuracy, address biases, and enhance user satisfaction.

Best Practices for Integrating OpenAI into Social Media Platforms

1. **Ethical Implementation**: Ensure transparency in how AI-driven recommendations are made. Users should have access to information about why specific content is prioritized and the ability to adjust their preferences.

2. **Customization Options**: Allow users to personalize their experience by adjusting algorithm settings, such as toggling between chronological feeds and curated recommendations.

3. **Regular Audits**: Conduct periodic evaluations of AI-generated content and recommendations to ensure fairness, inclusivity, and the absence of unintended biases.

4. **Scalable Infrastructure**: Deploy OpenAI models on robust, scalable platforms to handle large volumes of real-time data without compromising performance or user experience.

5. **Privacy Protection**: Prioritize user data privacy by employing encryption and ensuring compliance with data protection regulations

such as GDPR or CCPA.

Example Code for OpenAI Integration

Below is a simplified example of how OpenAI's GPT API can be integrated into a recommendation system:

import OpenAI.

```
# OpenAI API Key Setup
openai.api_key = "your_api_key_here"

# User Data for Content Recommendation
user_preferences = {
"interests": ["travel", "technology", "fitness"],
"recent_interactions": ["AI advancements", "best workout
routines"]
}

# Generating Content Suggestions
def generate_recommendations(user_data):
prompt = f"Based on the user's interests in {',
'.join(user_data['interests'])} and recent interactions with
{', '.join(user_data['recent_interactions'])}, suggest
personalized content topics."

response = openai.Completion.create(
engine="text-davinci-003",
prompt=prompt,
max_tokens=150
)

return response.choices[0].text.strip()

# Fetch and Display Recommendations
```

```
   recommendations =
generate_recommendations(user_preferences)
   print ("Recommended Content:", recommendations)
```

This script demonstrates how OpenAI's GPT API can analyze user interests and interactions to generate tailored content suggestions. Developers can adapt this framework to include additional parameters or integrate it with broader platform functionalities.

Moving Forward

Integrating OpenAI into social media platforms offers immense potential for enhancing user engagement, improving content personalization, and maintaining a positive online environment. By combining OpenAI's capabilities with ethical practices and robust infrastructure, organizations can address existing challenges while unlocking new opportunities for innovation and growth in the social media landscape.

The Ethics of Emotional Intelligence in Machines

The integration of emotional intelligence into artificial systems represents a significant leap in technology. Machines equipped with the capacity to interpret, respond to, and even simulate human emotions are redefining interactions across industries. From customer service bots to therapeutic AI, these systems aim to enhance engagement by recognizing and addressing the emotional states of their users. However, the rise of emotionally intelligent machines brings forth critical ethical considerations that require thoughtful examination.

One of the primary ethical concerns is the authenticity of emotional responses generated by machines. While an emotionally intelligent AI can simulate empathy, it lacks genuine understanding or experience of emotions. This raises questions about the morality of creating systems that mimic human affect without the underlying consciousness. Can interactions with such systems foster genuine connection, or do they risk misleading users into attributing human-like qualities to machines that are fundamentally devoid of emotions?

The use of emotionally intelligent systems also introduces potential risks related to manipulation. AI systems designed to gauge emotional states can potentially exploit this capability to influence behavior. For instance, a marketing chatbot might detect frustration in a user and leverage this information to push a sale. While such applications can increase efficiency and customer satisfaction, they also toe the line of ethical acceptability. Transparent practices and clear boundaries are essential to ensure that these technologies prioritize user well-being over profit.

Privacy is another significant consideration. For emotionally intelligent machines to function effectively, they require access to sensitive data, including voice tone, facial expressions, and contextual cues. This raises concerns about how such data is collected, stored, and utilized. Misuse or unauthorized access to this information could lead to severe consequences, including breaches of trust and exploitation. Ensuring robust data protection frameworks and obtaining informed consent are critical to addressing these concerns.

The deployment of emotionally intelligent AI in sensitive domains, such as mental health or education, demands even greater scrutiny. In therapy applications, for example, an AI system might provide emotional support to individuals struggling with loneliness or anxiety. While such systems can offer accessible and immediate assistance, they should never replace human professionals in scenarios requiring deep empathy and nuanced judgment. Striking the right balance between AI support and human involvement is crucial to avoid over-reliance on these systems in areas where human expertise is indispensable.

Furthermore, the development of emotionally intelligent machines must reflect diverse cultural and social norms. Emotions are deeply influenced by cultural contexts, and the interpretation of emotional cues varies widely across societies. An AI system trained on data from one cultural background may misinterpret or fail to recognize the emotional expressions of users from another. This underscores the need for inclusive datasets and culturally adaptive algorithms to ensure that these systems serve a global audience effectively and ethically.

The ethical development of emotionally intelligent AI also requires accountability. Developers and organizations must take responsibility for the actions and decisions of these systems. This involves conducting rigorous testing to identify and mitigate biases, as well as implementing clear protocols for addressing errors or misuse. Establishing accountability frameworks not only fosters trust but also ensures that these technologies are aligned with societal values.

Pablo Rodríguez (2023) emphasizes the transformative potential of AI in reshaping human interactions, particularly through systems that mimic emotional intelligence. He argues that while these systems can improve accessibility and foster new forms of connection, their deployment must be guided by ethical imperatives to prevent misuse and erosion of human dignity. Incorporating these insights into the design and implementation of emotionally intelligent AI ensures that technological advancements remain grounded in human-centered values.

Additionally, emotionally intelligent AI can play a pivotal role in disaster response and humanitarian efforts. For instance, these systems can detect distress signals in communication during crises, enabling faster and more targeted interventions. However, as Rodríguez (2023) notes, the application of such technologies must always be accompanied by transparent governance to avoid unintended consequences or exploitation in vulnerable scenarios.

The incorporation of emotional intelligence in machines offers immense potential to improve user experiences, foster meaningful interactions, and address complex challenges. However, the ethical implications cannot be overlooked. By prioritizing transparency, cultural sensitivity, user privacy, and accountability, developers can create systems that respect and enhance human dignity while leveraging the capabilities of emotional intelligence. As technology continues to evolve, it is our collective responsibility to ensure that these advancements contribute positively to society.

7 CHAPTER

HEALTH AND WELLNESS: AI AS A GUARDIAN ANGEL

Artificial intelligence is revolutionizing health and wellness, transforming medical science while empowering individuals to manage their physical and mental well-being. Acting as a "guardian angel," AI enables healthcare systems to become more initiative-taking, personalized, and efficient, ensuring timely and effective care for everyone.

One of AI's most significant contributions is its ability to predict and prevent health issues before they become critical. Wearable devices, such as smartwatches and fitness trackers, continuously monitor vital signs like heart rate, oxygen levels, and sleep patterns. These devices detect anomalies that could indicate underlying conditions, prompting users to seek medical attention. For example, AI-enhanced wearables can identify irregular heart rhythms, providing early warnings for conditions like atrial fibrillation, which, if untreated, could lead to severe complications. Beyond individual monitoring, AI systems analyze data from electronic health records and public health databases to identify patterns and predict disease outbreaks. This capability allows healthcare providers to allocate resources effectively and implement preventive measures to protect entire communities.

AI is also driving the era of personalized medicine, tailoring treatments to the unique genetic, environmental, and lifestyle factors of everyone. Machine learning algorithms process vast datasets to determine the most effective therapies for specific patient profiles. In oncology, for example, AI predicts how a patient's cancer will respond to various treatments, enabling clinicians to design targeted therapies with greater precision. Similarly, pharmacogenomics—the study of how genes influence drug responses—leverages AI to identify optimal dosages and minimize adverse reactions, ensuring safer and more effective care.

Mental health care is another area experiencing transformative advancements through AI. Virtual therapists, powered by natural language processing, engage users in meaningful conversations to assess mental states and offer coping strategies. Applications like Woebot and Wysa have shown remarkable success in delivering cognitive behavioral therapy techniques, helping reduce symptoms of anxiety and depression. Beyond virtual interactions, AI systems analyze behavioral data, such as changes in speech patterns or sleep habits, to detect early signs of mental health conditions. This initiative-taking approach enables early intervention, improving long-term outcomes and reducing the risk of worsening conditions.

In diagnostics, AI's ability to process vast amounts of information and detect subtle patterns is unmatched. Radiology exemplifies this, with AI-powered imaging tools identifying tumors, fractures, and infections with remarkable accuracy. By minimizing missed diagnoses, AI not only enhances patient outcomes but also reduces the workload for healthcare professionals. In primary care, AI chatbots and symptom checkers guide patients toward appropriate care pathways, reducing unnecessary visits to emergency rooms and clinics while optimizing resource allocation.

AI extends its influence beyond clinical settings to overall wellness and prevention. Personalized fitness apps use AI to design workout routines tailored to individual goals and fitness levels. Nutrition-focused platforms analyze dietary habits and provide recommendations to improve eating patterns, addressing health objectives like weight management or chronic condition control. In workplaces, AI analyzes employee health data to suggest interventions that enhance collective well-being, such as stress management programs or ergonomic adjustments, fostering healthier and more productive environments.

While AI's potential in health and wellness is vast, it also raises ethical and privacy concerns. The collection and analysis of sensitive health data require stringent security and transparency standards. Patient consent and compliance with regulations like GDPR and HIPAA are critical to maintaining trust. Moreover, addressing bias in AI algorithms is essential to ensure equitable care for all populations, regardless of race, gender, or socioeconomic background. Diverse and representative datasets are necessary to avoid perpetuating disparities in healthcare.

The integration of AI into health and wellness systems represents a future where care is both efficient and compassionate. By combining the precision and scalability of AI with the empathy and expertise of healthcare professionals, a balanced approach can be achieved. AI acts as a guardian angel, guiding individuals and communities toward healthier, more fulfilling lives while preserving the human touch that defines quality care.

The integration of artificial intelligence into health and wellness has set the stage for groundbreaking advancements, but its full potential is far from realized. Emerging innovations promise to further transform how we approach healthcare, prevention, and personal well-being. These future technologies, driven by AI, aim to address persistent challenges while opening new avenues for medical and wellness applications that prioritize precision, accessibility, and individual empowerment.

One of the most promising areas of development is AI-powered nanotechnology. These nanoscale systems, guided by machine learning algorithms, are envisioned as game changers in drug delivery and disease treatment. By navigating through the human body with unparalleled precision, AI-driven nanobots could identify and target specific cells or tissues, such as cancerous tumors, while leaving healthy cells untouched. This targeted approach minimizes side effects and enhances treatment efficacy, especially for complex conditions like cancer, neurodegenerative diseases, and autoimmune disorders. Beyond treatment, such nanotechnology could also assist in real-time diagnostics by collecting and transmitting critical biomarker data, enabling early detection of diseases that would otherwise go unnoticed.

Another frontier lies in brain-computer interfaces (BCIs) augmented with AI. These systems aim to establish direct communication pathways between the brain and external devices, offering transformative solutions for individuals with disabilities. AI-powered BCIs could restore mobility for those with paralysis by interpreting neural signals and translating them into actionable commands for robotic limbs or exoskeletons. Similarly, they hold promise for improving cognitive function in individuals with neurodegenerative conditions like Alzheimer's or Parkinson's. Future advancements may even enable the development of learning systems that adapt in real-time to the user's brain activity, facilitating faster skill acquisition and cognitive enhancement.

In the realm of mental health, AI's capacity for emotional intelligence is expected to reach new heights. Next-generation virtual therapists will leverage advanced natural language processing to engage users in deeply empathetic and nuanced conversations. By analyzing vocal tones, facial expressions, and behavioral patterns, these systems could offer tailored support that rivals human interaction. Additionally, AI could be integrated into wearable devices to monitor physiological indicators of stress or anxiety, providing immediate interventions such as breathing exercises, mindfulness prompts, or alerts to seek professional help.

The convergence of AI with augmented reality (AR) and virtual reality (VR) is set to redefine therapeutic practices and rehabilitation. AI-enhanced AR systems could guide patients through physical therapy exercises with real-time feedback on posture, movement, and progress. This personalized approach ensures adherence to recovery plans while minimizing the risk of reinjury. In mental health, VR environments powered by AI may create immersive simulations designed to reduce anxiety, manage chronic pain, or assist individuals in overcoming trauma through controlled exposure therapy.

AI's role in preventive care is also poised for significant expansion. Personalized wellness platforms will become more sophisticated, integrating real-time health data from wearables with environmental and behavioral insights to offer actionable recommendations. For instance, AI systems could predict the likelihood of developing chronic conditions based on lifestyle patterns and provide tailored interventions to mitigate those risks. These platforms may also coordinate with healthcare providers to deliver timely reminders for vaccinations, screenings, or routine check-ups, ensuring that preventive care remains a priority.

The future of AI in global health equity holds immense potential. By leveraging AI to analyze population health data, governments and organizations can identify underserved regions and allocate resources more effectively. AI-driven telemedicine platforms equipped with real-time translation and diagnostic capabilities could bring quality healthcare to remote or impoverished areas, bridging gaps in access and improving outcomes on a global scale.

Ethical considerations will play a pivotal role in shaping these advancements. The integration of AI in sensitive areas like neural interfaces, emotional intelligence systems, and real-time health monitoring raises questions about privacy, consent, and bias. Ensuring that these systems operate transparently and inclusively will be crucial for building public trust and maximizing their societal impact. Robust regulatory frameworks and interdisciplinary collaboration will be essential to navigate these complexities responsibly.

As AI continues to evolve, its potential to revolutionize health and wellness is boundless. By focusing on innovation that prioritizes personalization, accessibility, and ethical integrity, AI can serve as a catalyst for a future where healthcare is not only more advanced but also deeply human-centered. These advancements promise to empower individuals, enhance the capabilities of healthcare professionals, and create a more equitable global health landscape, ensuring that the benefits of AI-driven technology are felt universally.

Wearables and Predictive Health Monitoring

The advent of wearable technology has significantly transformed the landscape of health monitoring, enabled real-time insights and fostered a more proactive approach to healthcare. Wearables, equipped with advanced sensors and artificial intelligence (AI) capabilities, provide continuous data on vital signs, activity levels, and other health metrics. These innovations have not only improved individual wellness management but have also paved the way for predictive health monitoring, where potential health issues can be identified before they become critical.

Modern wearable devices, such as smartwatches, fitness trackers, and biosensors, are designed to monitor parameters like heart rate, blood oxygen levels, sleep patterns, and physical activity. These devices employ machine learning algorithms to analyze trends and detect anomalies. For instance, wearable electrocardiogram (ECG) monitors can identify irregular heart rhythms, offering early warnings for conditions like atrial fibrillation. Such early detection is crucial in preventing complications such as stroke or heart failure, ensuring timely medical intervention (Benedict et al., 2021).

One of the most promising applications of wearables lies in chronic disease management. For individuals with diabetes, continuous glucose monitors (CGMs) track blood sugar levels and provide actionable insights to maintain optimal control. These devices integrate with smartphone applications to deliver alerts and recommendations, helping users make informed decisions about their diet, exercise, and medication. Similarly, for patients with respiratory conditions, wearable spirometers track lung function, enabling clinicians to adjust treatment plans based on real-time data.

The role of predictive health monitoring extends beyond individual care to population health management. By aggregating anonymized data from wearable devices, researchers and healthcare providers can identify trends and predict disease outbreaks. For example, wearable data collected during the COVID-19 pandemic helped researchers understand early symptoms and track the virus's spread, illustrating the potential of these technologies in managing public health crises (Mishra et al., 2020).

Wearables are also driving advancements in mental health care. Devices equipped with electrodermal activity (EDA) sensors can detect stress levels by measuring skin conductance, while others monitor sleep quality and its impact on mental well-being. These insights empower users to adopt stress-reduction techniques and seek professional support when necessary. AI-enhanced wearables, like smart rings or bracelets, even integrate mindfulness prompts and breathing exercises, offering real-time interventions to improve emotional health.

Despite their transformative potential, wearables face challenges that must be addressed to maximize their impact. Data privacy is a primary concern, as these devices collect sensitive health information. Ensuring compliance with regulations like the General Data Protection Regulation (GDPR) and the Health Insurance Portability and Accountability Act (HIPAA) is essential to protect user data and maintain trust. Additionally, the accuracy and reliability of wearable sensors vary across devices, underscoring the need for standardization and rigorous validation.

Looking ahead, the future of wearables in predictive health monitoring is poised for further innovation. Advances in nanotechnology could lead to ultra-thin, flexible sensors that integrate seamlessly with the skin, providing continuous monitoring without discomfort. AI will play a critical role in enhancing predictive capabilities, enabling devices to not only identify potential issues but also recommend personalized interventions. For instance, wearables may soon predict the onset of migraines based on subtle physiological changes, allowing users to take preventive measures.

Collaborations between tech companies, healthcare providers, and researchers will be vital in driving these advancements. Partnerships like those between Apple and leading health institutions demonstrate the potential of combining technological expertise with clinical knowledge to create impactful solutions. By prioritizing accuracy, accessibility, and ethical considerations, wearable technology can continue to revolutionize health monitoring and contribute to a healthier, more informed society.

Mental Health Apps and Virtual Therapists

The growing prevalence of mental health challenges has driven a surge in technological innovations aimed at improving accessibility and effectiveness of mental health care. Among these advancements, mental health apps and virtual therapists have emerged as transformative tools, bridging gaps in traditional care models and empowering individuals to take initiative-taking steps toward emotional well-being. By leveraging artificial intelligence (AI) and machine learning, these solutions provide personalized, scalable, and often cost-effective support.

Mental health apps have rapidly gained traction due to their convenience and versatility. Platforms such as **Calm**, **Headspace**, and **Better Help** offer users resources ranging from guided meditations and stress management techniques to virtual counseling sessions with licensed professionals. These apps enable individuals to access care on their own terms, removing barriers such as geographical limitations, scheduling constraints, and social stigma. Many of these tools integrate AI algorithms to provide tailored recommendations, such as customized mindfulness exercises or mood-tracking insights, ensuring a user-centric approach.

Virtual therapists, powered by AI, take mental health support a step further by simulating human-like interactions. Applications like **Woebot** and **Wysa** employ natural language processing to engage users in therapeutic conversations, offering coping strategies and emotional validation. These virtual agents are particularly effective for addressing mild to moderate mental health concerns, such as anxiety, depression, and stress. By analyzing patterns in user input, virtual therapists can adapt their responses, creating a sense of empathy and understanding that fosters trust and engagement.

The scalability of mental health apps and virtual therapists addresses a critical need in global mental health care. According to the World Health Organization (WHO), there is a significant shortage of mental health professionals worldwide, leaving millions without access to adequate support. Digital tools can bridge this gap by reaching underserved populations, including those in remote or low-income areas.

For instance, AI-powered platforms equipped with multilingual capabilities can deliver culturally sensitive care, ensuring inclusivity and relevance across diverse user bases.

Moreover, these technologies facilitate continuous monitoring and early intervention. Apps equipped with mood trackers, journaling features, and biometric integrations enable users to track their emotional and physiological states over time. For example, an app may analyze data from a wearable device to detect signs of elevated stress, prompting the user to engage in relaxation exercises or seek professional help. This initiative-taking approach empowers individuals to manage their mental health more effectively, reducing the likelihood of crises and improving long-term outcomes.

Despite their numerous benefits, mental health apps and virtual therapists are not without limitations. One major concern is data privacy. Given the sensitive nature of mental health information, developers must ensure that these platforms comply with stringent security protocols, such as encryption and adherence to regulations like GDPR and HIPAA. Transparency in how data is collected, stored, and used is essential for maintaining user trust.

Another challenge lies in ensuring the efficacy and reliability of these tools. While many apps are evidence-based and developed in collaboration with mental health professionals, others lack scientific validation. Users must navigate a crowded marketplace to identify credible options, highlighting the need for clearer industry standards and certification processes.

The integration of mental health apps and virtual therapists with traditional care models offers promising avenues for comprehensive support. Hybrid approaches, where digital tools complement in-person therapy, can enhance treatment outcomes by providing continuous access to resources between sessions. For instance, a therapist may recommend specific app-based exercises to reinforce coping skills discussed during a session, fostering a more cohesive care experience.

Looking ahead, advancements in AI and wearable technology are expected to further revolutionize mental health care. Future apps may incorporate real-time emotional recognition, using facial expressions, voice tone, or physiological data to provide even more tailored interventions. Additionally, the integration of virtual reality (VR) with AI could create immersive therapeutic experiences, such as exposure therapy for phobias or stress-reduction environments, offering innovative ways to address complex mental health needs.

Mental health apps and virtual therapists represent a change in basic assumptions in how we approach emotional well-being. By combining technological innovation with human empathy, these tools have the potential to democratize mental health care, making it accessible, personalized, and effective for individuals worldwide. However, achieving this vision requires ongoing collaboration among technologists, clinicians, and policymakers to ensure that these solutions uphold the highest standards of quality, ethics, and inclusivity.

Mental Health Apps and Virtual Therapists

The growing prevalence of mental health challenges has driven a surge in technological innovations aimed at improving accessibility and effectiveness of mental health care. Among these advancements, mental health apps and virtual therapists have emerged as transformative tools, bridging gaps in traditional care models and empowering individuals to take initiative-taking steps toward emotional well-being. By leveraging artificial intelligence (AI) and machine learning, these solutions provide personalized, scalable, and often cost-effective support.

Mental health apps have rapidly gained traction due to their convenience and versatility. Platforms such as **Calm**, **Headspace**, and **Better Help** offer users resources ranging from guided meditations and stress management techniques to virtual counseling sessions with licensed professionals. These apps enable individuals to access care on their own terms, removing barriers such as geographical limitations, scheduling constraints, and social stigma. Many of these tools integrate AI algorithms to provide tailored recommendations, such as customized mindfulness exercises or mood-tracking insights, ensuring a user-centric approach.

Virtual therapists, powered by AI, take mental health support a step further by simulating human-like interactions. Applications like **Woebot** and **Wysa** employ natural language processing to engage users in therapeutic conversations, offering coping strategies and emotional validation. These virtual agents are particularly effective for addressing mild to moderate mental health concerns, such as anxiety, depression, and stress. By analyzing patterns in user input, virtual therapists can adapt their responses, creating a sense of empathy and understanding that fosters trust and engagement.

The scalability of mental health apps and virtual therapists addresses a critical need in global mental health care. According to the World Health Organization (WHO), there is a significant shortage of mental health professionals worldwide, leaving millions without access to adequate support. Digital tools can bridge this gap by reaching underserved populations, including those in remote or low-income areas. For instance, AI-powered platforms equipped with multilingual capabilities can deliver culturally sensitive care, ensuring inclusivity and relevance across diverse user bases.

Moreover, these technologies facilitate continuous monitoring and early intervention. Apps equipped with mood trackers, journaling features, and biometric integrations enable users to track their emotional and physiological states over time. For example, an app may analyze data from a wearable device to detect signs of elevated stress, prompting the user to engage in relaxation exercises or seek professional help. This initiative-taking approach empowers individuals to manage their mental health more effectively, reducing the likelihood of crises and improving long-term outcomes.

Despite their numerous benefits, mental health apps and virtual therapists are not without limitations. One major concern is data privacy. Given the sensitive nature of mental health information, developers must ensure that these platforms comply with stringent security protocols, such as encryption and adherence to regulations like GDPR and HIPAA. Transparency in how data is collected, stored, and used is essential for maintaining user trust.

Another challenge lies in ensuring the efficacy and reliability of these tools. While many apps are evidence-based and developed in collaboration with mental health professionals, others lack scientific validation. Users must navigate a crowded marketplace to identify credible options, highlighting the need for clearer industry standards and certification processes.

The integration of mental health apps and virtual therapists with traditional care models offers promising avenues for comprehensive support. Hybrid approaches, where digital tools complement in-person therapy, can enhance treatment outcomes by providing continuous access to resources between sessions. For instance, a therapist may recommend specific app-based exercises to reinforce coping skills discussed during a session, fostering a more cohesive care experience.

Looking ahead, advancements in AI and wearable technology are expected to further revolutionize mental health care. Future apps may incorporate real-time emotional recognition, using facial expressions, voice tone, or physiological data to provide even more tailored interventions. Additionally, the integration of virtual reality (VR) with AI could create immersive therapeutic experiences, such as exposure therapy for phobias or stress-reduction environments, offering innovative ways to address complex mental health needs.

Mental health apps and virtual therapists represent a change in thinking in how we approach emotional well-being. By combining technological innovation with human empathy, these tools have the potential to democratize mental health care, making it accessible, personalized, and effective for individuals worldwide. However, achieving this vision requires ongoing collaboration among technologists, clinicians, and policymakers to ensure that these solutions uphold the highest standards of quality, ethics, and inclusivity.

Future Mental AI

The rapid evolution of mental health technology has provided invaluable tools for addressing emotional well-being, yet the potential of mental health apps and virtual therapists remains far from fully realized. As artificial intelligence (AI) and related technologies advance, new opportunities emerge to further personalize, innovate, and expand access to mental health care. Exploring these possibilities requires identifying existing gaps and envisioning what could enhance current capabilities. One of the primary areas for growth is improving the emotional intelligence of virtual therapists. Current systems, such as Woebot and Wysa, excel in recognizing user input and responding with appropriate pre-designed interventions. However, their capacity for nuanced emotional understanding remains limited. Future developments could integrate advanced sentiment analysis tools, combining natural language processing with real-time monitoring of vocal tone, facial expressions, and physiological data to provide more empathetic and context-aware responses. These improvements would allow virtual therapists to respond not only to what users say but also to how they feel in the moment.

While many apps aim to serve global audiences, few are genuinely adapted to diverse cultural and societal contexts. Mental health is deeply influenced by cultural values, language, and social norms. Expanding datasets to include underrepresented populations and training AI systems to recognize culturally specific idioms, stressors, and coping mechanisms could make these tools more inclusive and effective. Multilingual support with localized content would further reduce barriers, ensuring equitable access across regions. Current mental health apps are primarily designed for routine care or low to moderate mental health challenges. There remains an untapped potential for apps that can intervene effectively during crises. AI-powered systems could integrate with emergency response services, alerting mental health professionals or trusted contacts when a user exhibits signs of acute distress, such as suicidal ideation or severe anxiety attacks. Combining these capabilities with wearable technology could enhance real-time crisis detection by monitoring heart rate variability, stress hormones, or other biological markers of distress.

The constructive interaction between mental health apps and wearable devices holds enormous promise. Future applications could leverage data from smartwatches, fitness trackers, or even advanced neural interfaces to monitor users' physical and emotional states continuously. For instance, a wearable might detect increased stress levels through skin conductance and prompt the user—via their app— to engage in calming exercises or connect with a virtual therapist. Such integrations could transform mental health care into a dynamic, always-on support system. The intersection of AI and virtual reality (VR) has the potential to redefine therapeutic experiences. Immersive environments could be tailored to individual needs, enabling exposure therapy for conditions like phobias, PTSD, or social anxiety in controlled, AI-supervised settings. Virtual therapists within these environments could guide users through scenarios designed to build resilience and confidence. For example, a person with a fear of public speaking might practice in a realistic VR auditorium, receiving real-time feedback from an AI coach on tone, pacing, and audience engagement.

Future apps could incorporate AI-driven personalization to an unprecedented degree. By analyzing user history, preferences, and progress, these systems could design highly specific therapy plans that adapt dynamically over time. This might include recommending new therapeutic approaches, identifying which techniques are most effective for a particular user, or integrating feedback from human therapists to refine care strategies. As these technologies evolve, building and maintaining user trust will be paramount. Transparency about how data is collected, stored, and used must become a standard feature of all mental health apps. Advances in secure AI systems, such as those utilizing differential privacy, could help ensure that sensitive mental health data remains confidential while still enabling robust analytics. Developing ethical frameworks that prioritize user autonomy and consent will be critical in fostering widespread adoption and long-term success.

While mental health apps have expanded access to care, significant gaps remain for individuals in low-income or rural areas without reliable internet or smartphone access. Addressing this disparity requires developing lightweight applications that function offline or in areas with limited connectivity. Partnerships with government agencies or NGOs could facilitate distribution and subsidization of these tools, ensuring broader reach. The field must also emphasize rigorous validation of these technologies through peer-reviewed studies and clinical trials. While many apps claim to be evidence-based, not all undergo the same level of scrutiny as traditional therapeutic interventions. Collaborations with academic institutions and mental health organizations can establish benchmarks for efficacy and safety, ensuring that users benefit from scientifically validated tools. The future of mental health apps and virtual therapists lies in their ability to integrate seamlessly into daily life while offering highly personalized and culturally sensitive care. By leveraging advances in AI, wearables, and immersive technologies, these tools could become indispensable allies in addressing global mental health challenges. However, achieving this vision requires collaboration between technologists, clinicians, and policymakers to create solutions that are ethical, inclusive, and grounded in evidence. As the field progresses, mental health care could become more accessible, effective, and transformative than ever before.

8 CHAPTER

THE DARK SIDE OF AI: RISKS AND CHALLENGES

Artificial intelligence, with its transformative potential, has undoubtedly revolutionized industries and redefined the way we live and work. However, alongside its advancements lies a darker, more complex side that demands critical examination. The risks and challenges posed by AI are multifaceted, spanning ethical, social, economic, and security domains. Recognizing and addressing these issues is essential to ensure that AI serves humanity responsibly and equitably.

One of the most pressing concerns is the issue of bias embedded in AI systems. These algorithms, trained on historical data, often reflect and amplify societal prejudices. From recruitment tools favoring certain demographics to facial recognition systems struggling to identify individuals from diverse racial backgrounds, AI's capacity to perpetuate discrimination has significant consequences. This problem arises from training datasets that lack diversity or are skewed by historical inequities. Without rigorous oversight and the implementation of inclusive datasets, AI risks entrenching systemic biases rather than alleviating them.

Privacy is another critical challenge associated with AI. The data-driven nature of these systems means they rely on vast amounts of personal information to function effectively. This creates significant vulnerabilities, as sensitive data can be misused, breached, or exploited. For instance, AI-powered surveillance systems raise concerns about mass monitoring and the erosion of individual privacy. Similarly, predictive analytics in healthcare or marketing often push the boundaries of ethical data usage, prompting questions about consent and the limits of algorithmic decision-making.

Security risks also loom large in the realm of AI. Adversarial attacks, where malicious actors manipulate AI systems to produce incorrect outputs, have demonstrated the fragility of even the most sophisticated models. In autonomous vehicles, for example, adversarial inputs could cause navigation systems to misinterpret road signs, leading to potentially catastrophic outcomes. Cybersecurity threats targeting AI systems amplify the stakes, as compromised models can disrupt critical infrastructure or manipulate public opinion.

The economic implications of AI present additional challenges. Automation driven by AI threatens to displace significant segments of the workforce, particularly in industries reliant on repetitive or manual tasks. While AI creates new opportunities, the transition may leave many individuals and communities unprepared, exacerbating inequality and social unrest. Addressing this requires an initiative-taking approach to reskilling and education, ensuring that the benefits of AI are distributed equitably.

AI's role in spreading misinformation and deepfakes is another area of concern. With the ability to generate hyper-realistic fake content, AI has been weaponized to manipulate public opinion, undermine trust in institutions, and exacerbate political polarization. Deepfake technology, capable of creating convincing but false images and videos, poses risks to personal reputations, elections, and global security. The proliferation of such content challenges society's ability to discern truth from fabrication, requiring robust tools and policies to combat its misuse.

Ethical dilemmas surrounding autonomous systems further underscore the dark side of AI. In military applications, for instance, autonomous drones and weaponized AI raise questions about accountability and the potential for unintended harm. Who is responsible when an AI-driven system makes a fatal error? Similar concerns arise in healthcare, where algorithmic decisions can directly impact patient outcomes. Ensuring that AI systems align with ethical principles requires not only technical safeguards but also a framework for accountability and governance.

Finally, the concentration of AI development and resources in a few powerful entities—whether governments or tech giants—poses a risk to global equity. This concentration can exacerbate existing power imbalances, allowing a select few to dictate the trajectory of AI advancements and their applications. Such dynamics threaten to marginalize smaller nations, organizations, and communities, undermining the democratizing potential of technology.

To address these challenges, a multifaceted approach is essential. Developers must prioritize transparency in AI systems, ensuring that algorithms are explainable and accountable. Policymakers should establish robust regulations that balance innovation with ethical safeguards, addressing concerns about privacy, bias, and security. Collaboration between governments, industry, and academia is crucial to developing standards that reflect shared values and principles. Education and public awareness also play vital roles in empowering individuals to engage with AI critically and responsibly.

While the risks and challenges of AI are significant, they are not insurmountable. By confronting these issues with foresight and collective effort, society can shape AI to be a force for good, minimizing its darker aspects and maximizing its potential to contribute positively to humanity.

Bias in algorithms refers to systematic errors or prejudices embedded in automated systems that lead to unfair or unintended outcomes. These biases often arise from the data used to train the algorithms, the design decisions made during development, or the broader societal and cultural influences reflected in the system.

Types of Algorithmic Bias

Algorithmic bias manifests in numerous ways, depending on the context and application:

1. **Data Bias**:
   o Algorithms are trained on datasets, which may not represent the full diversity of real-world scenarios. For example, facial recognition systems trained on predominantly white faces have been shown to perform poorly when recognizing individuals with darker skin tones.

2. **Selection Bias**:
   o This occurs when the training data does not adequately cover all necessary scenarios, leading to skewed results. For instance, a hiring algorithm trained predominantly on male resumes might favor male candidates, perpetuating gender imbalances.

3. **Confirmation Bias**:
   o Algorithms may reinforce existing patterns in the data. For example, if historical loan data shows a preference for granting loans to individuals from affluent areas, the algorithm might systematically disadvantage applicants from less privileged backgrounds.

4. **Interaction Bias**:
   o This occurs when users influence an algorithm's behavior during its use. For example, biased user inputs in a search engine can lead to biased results.

Causes of Algorithmic Bias

1. **Historical Inequities in Data**:
   - o Algorithms often reflect societal biases because they are trained on historical data, which may contain prejudices based on race, gender, or socio-economic status.

2. **Inadequate Diversity in Development Teams**:
   - o Lack of diversity among developers can lead to blind spots, as individuals may unconsciously embed their biases into the systems they create.

3. **Imbalanced Data Sets**:
   - o Overrepresentation or underrepresentation of certain groups in training data can skew an algorithm's performance.

4. **Unintended Design Choices**:
   - o Decisions such as feature selection, weighting, and model architecture can inadvertently favor certain outcomes over others.

Examples of Bias in Real-World Applications

1. **Facial Recognition Technology**:
   - o Studies have shown significant discrepancies in error rates for different demographic groups, leading to concerns about its use in law enforcement and public surveillance.

2. **Hiring Algorithms**:
   - o Automated systems used for screening job applicants have been found to favor male candidates, as they often

learn from past hiring decisions biased against women.

3. **Healthcare Algorithms**:
   - o Some healthcare systems prioritize care based on cost rather than medical necessity, disproportionately affecting lower-income or minority groups.

4. **Social Media Platforms**:
   - o Content moderation algorithms may disproportionately target certain languages or cultural expressions, leading to censorship or reduced visibility for minority groups.

Mitigating Algorithmic Bias

1. **Diverse and Inclusive Data**:
   - o Ensuring datasets are representative of all demographic groups and regularly updating them to reflect changes in society.

2. **Transparency in Algorithm Design**:
   - o Openly documenting how algorithms are built and how decisions are made can help identify potential biases.

3. **Bias Testing and Auditing**:
   - o Regularly evaluating algorithms for biases using controlled tests can uncover and address issues before deployment.

4. **Inclusive Development Teams**:
   - o Involving diverse perspectives in the design and testing phases can help uncover blind spots and reduce unintentional bias.

5. **Regulatory Frameworks**:

o Governments and organizations can implement guidelines to ensure fairness, accountability, and transparency in algorithmic systems.

Ethical and Social Implications

Bias in algorithms has significant ethical and societal implications, as these systems increasingly influence critical decisions in areas such as hiring, lending, policing, and healthcare. If left unchecked, algorithmic bias can exacerbate inequalities, perpetuate stereotypes, and erode trust in technology.

The Path Forward

Addressing bias in algorithms requires a multifaceted approach involving technical innovation, ethical oversight, and societal engagement. By fostering transparency, accountability, and inclusivity, we can build systems that are not only intelligent but also fair and equitable for all.

The Importance of Diverse Perspectives

Bias often stems from homogeneous perspectives during the development process. By including individuals from diverse backgrounds—culturally, socially, and professionally—organizations can:

- Identify potential blind spots.
- Ensure systems cater to a wider range of users.
- Create products that reflect the diversity of the real world.

For example, inclusive teams are better equipped to detect biases in datasets or design decisions that might otherwise go unnoticed.

Technical Approaches to Mitigate Bias

Technologists have developed several methods to reduce algorithmic bias, including:

1. **Preprocessing Data**:
   - Cleaning and balancing datasets to ensure they fairly represent all relevant groups. For example, data augmentation can increase the representation of underrepresented groups.

2. **Fairness-Aware Algorithms**:
   - Developing algorithms explicitly designed to account for fairness. Techniques such as reweighting or adversarial training can adjust models to produce equitable outcomes.

3. **Post-Processing Results**:
   - Modifying algorithm outputs to ensure fairness, even if the underlying model or data is biased. For instance, thresholds can be adjusted to equalize error rates across demographic groups.

4. **Bias Testing Tools**:
   - Tools like IBM's AI Fairness 360 or Google's What-If Tool allow developers to evaluate the fairness of their systems and explore the impact of distinctive design decisions.

The Role of Education

Education plays a pivotal role in mitigating algorithmic bias. Developers, policymakers, and the public must be informed about:

- **How algorithms work:**
  - Understanding the basics of machine learning and data science can help demystify algorithms and highlight potential sources of bias.

- **The impact of biases:**
  - Awareness of how biased algorithms can perpetuate discrimination, or inequality can drive demand for fairer systems.
  -

- **Ethical AI Development:**
  - Incorporating ethics into technical curricula ensures future developers prioritize fairness and accountability.

In our increasingly interconnected and technology-driven world, dependence on automated systems, artificial intelligence, and digital solutions is becoming both an enabler and a risk. While these tools empower industries, streamline processes, and elevate human capabilities, they also expose us to vulnerabilities that arise when reliance evolves into overdependence. The threat of overdependence is not a distant hypothetical; it is a present and growing concern with implications across societal, economic, and individual dimensions.

Defining Overdependence

Overdependence occurs when systems or individuals rely excessively on a single tool, process, or resource to the extent that their ability to function independently is compromised. This phenomenon can manifest in various contexts:

- **Technological Overdependence**: Relying heavily on AI systems, automation, or software to perform tasks that were traditionally overseen by humans.
- **Systemic Overdependence**: When an entire industry or sector becomes overly reliant on a single point of failure, such as a key supplier or technology.
- **Cognitive Overdependence**: The erosion of critical thinking and critical thinking skills due to constant reliance on external aids like search engines or digital assistants.

The Roots of Overdependence

1. **Convenience and Efficiency**: The pursuit of efficiency often encourages the adoption of automated solutions. Over time, convenience can evolve into complacency, as individuals and organizations defer decision-making and problem-solving to automated systems.

2. **Perceived Reliability**: Advanced systems, particularly those driven by AI, often outperform humans in specific tasks. This consistent performance fosters trust, which can lead to uncritical

reliance.

3. **Cost Pressures**: Automation often reduces operational costs, incentivizing businesses to automate more processes. However, this financial gain can mask the risk of losing human expertise and flexibility.

4. **Lack of Awareness**: Many users are unaware of the risks associated with overdependence until a failure occurs, at which point the consequences can be severe.

The Risks of Overdependence

1. **Systemic Failures**: Overdependence on a single technology or provider creates a bottleneck for systemic failure. A cyberattack, software glitch, or geopolitical disruption can paralyze entire networks or industries.

2. **Loss of Human Expertise**: When humans rely excessively on automated systems, they risk losing the skills necessary to intervene or innovate when those systems fail. For example, overdependence on autopilot technology in aviation has raised concerns about pilots' manual flying skills.

3. **Reduced Resilience**: Resilience comes from redundancy and adaptability. Overdependence erodes both by centralizing reliance on a singular solution, leaving systems unprepared for disruptions.

4. **Ethical and Social Implications**: Excessive reliance on algorithms can perpetuate biases, as humans may accept machine outputs uncritically. Additionally, societal inequalities can deepen when overdependence on advanced technologies leaves certain populations excluded.

Real-World Examples of Overdependence

1. **Global Supply Chains**: The COVID-19 pandemic exposed vulnerabilities in global supply chains reliant on just-in-time manufacturing and limited suppliers. Industries faced severe disruptions due to a lack of diversification and preparedness for systemic shocks.

2. **Cybersecurity Threats**: Overdependence on interconnected digital systems makes organizations vulnerable to cyberattacks. For instance, ransomware attacks have paralyzed hospitals, municipalities, and major corporations.

3. **Financial Algorithms**: The 2010 "Flash Crash" highlighted the risks of overdependence on high-frequency trading algorithms, which triggered a rapid and chaotic stock market plunge in a matter of minutes.

4. **Education and Learning**: Increasing reliance on search engines and learning apps has raised concerns about diminishing critical thinking and problem-solving abilities, particularly in younger generations.

Mitigating the Risks of Overdependence

Addressing the threat of overdependence requires a proactive and multi-faceted approach:

1. **Building Redundancies**: Diversifying suppliers, technologies, and resources reduces the impact of a single point of failure. Organizations should maintain contingency plans and regularly evaluate their dependencies.

2. **Investing in Human Expertise**: Continuous training and development ensure that human skills remain sharp, complementing automated systems rather than being replaced by them.

3. **Implementing Ethical AI Practices**: Ensuring transparency, accountability, and fairness in AI systems prevents blind reliance. Users should be educated on the limitations and biases of algorithms.

4. **Promoting Digital Literacy**: Individuals should be equipped with the skills to critically evaluate digital tools and understand their limitations. Schools, workplaces, and communities can play a role in fostering this awareness.

5. **Scenario Planning and Stress Testing**: Organizations must regularly evaluate their systems against various failure scenarios. This helps identify vulnerabilities and prepares teams to respond effectively.

The Role of Accountability

Governments, businesses, and individuals must share responsibility in addressing overdependence. Governments can establish regulatory frameworks to promote transparency and resilience, while businesses can prioritize sustainable and ethical practices. At an individual level, fostering a culture of curiosity and critical thinking can prevent complacency.

A Balanced Approach

The solution is not to reject technology but to use it responsibly. By embracing a balanced approach that combines the strengths of human intuition and creativity with the precision and efficiency of machines, we can leverage technology while minimizing the risks of overdependence.

The threat of overdependence is a cautionary tale in our pursuit of progress. As we integrate technology deeper into our lives, we must remain vigilant about its limitations and risks. By fostering awareness, resilience, and adaptability, we can ensure that our relationship with technology remains a partnership—one that amplifies human potential without   diminishing   it.

9 CHAPTER

LOOKING AHEAD: THE FUTURE OF HUMAN-AI COLLABORATION

The relationship between humans and artificial intelligence (AI) is evolving rapidly, shaping a future where collaboration rather than competition will define our coexistence. As AI systems become increasingly sophisticated, the focus shifts from what machines can do independently to how they can complement human strengths and mitigate human limitations. The future of human-AI collaboration is not just about leveraging technology for efficiency; it is about forging a partnership that amplifies creativity, adaptability, and problem-solving across domains.

At the core of this collaboration lies the principle of synergy. Humans bring intuition, emotional intelligence, and the ability to navigate ambiguity—qualities that machines, despite their computational power, cannot replicate. Conversely, AI offers precision, scalability, and the ability to process vast amounts of data far beyond human capacity. Together, these complementary strengths create opportunities for innovation that neither could achieve alone. This collaboration has already begun to reshape industries, from healthcare to education, and its potential continues to expand as the technology matures.

In healthcare, for example, AI-driven diagnostic tools are becoming indispensable. Algorithms trained on millions of medical images can identify patterns that escape the human eye, leading to earlier and more accurate diagnoses. However, the ultimate decision-making remains in the hands of physicians, whose expertise contextualizes AI-generated insights within the complexities of patient care. The same holds true in other fields: architects use AI to optimize designs, but the vision and creativity that define their work remain human-driven. Similarly, educators harness AI to personalize learning experiences, yet the empathy and mentorship that shape education are uniquely human qualities.

For human-AI collaboration to thrive, trust is paramount. Trust is built not just on the reliability and transparency of AI systems but also on the assurance that these systems are designed with human values at their core. This requires a commitment to ethical development, where biases are identified and addressed, and where decision-making processes are explainable. Transparency fosters confidence, enabling users to understand how AI reaches its conclusions and allowing them to interact with the technology as informed partners rather than passive recipients.

The workplace is set to undergo significant transformation as human-

AI collaboration deepens. Rather than replacing jobs, AI will redefine them, automating repetitive tasks while freeing humans to focus on more complex, strategic, and creative responsibilities. This shift will demand a reimagining of skills and roles, emphasizing adaptability, critical thinking, and the ability to work effectively alongside machines. The education system must play a pivotal role in preparing future generations for this reality, integrating technical proficiency with a solid foundation in ethics and interpersonal skills.

However, the future of human-AI collaboration is not without its challenges. The rapid pace of AI development raises questions about accessibility and equity. If only a select few have access to advanced AI tools, disparities could deepen, exacerbating societal divides. To counteract this, governments, organizations, and communities must work together to democratize access to AI technologies, ensuring that the benefits are shared broadly. Additionally, frameworks for regulation and oversight will be crucial in maintaining accountability, preventing misuse, and safeguarding the public interest.

As we look ahead, the narrative of human-AI collaboration must emphasize partnership rather than domination. AI is a tool, and like any tool, its value depends on how it is used. The responsibility for shaping this future rests with humans—developers, policymakers, and users— who must prioritize principles of fairness, inclusivity, and sustainability. By designing systems that enhance human potential and address societal challenges, we can ensure that AI becomes a force for good, driving progress without compromising our values.

The future of human-AI collaboration is filled with promise. It represents a shift from seeing technology as merely an instrument to viewing it as a collaborator in solving the complex challenges of our time. Whether addressing climate change, advancing medical research, or enhancing education, the fusion of human ingenuity and artificial intelligence offers a path forward that is both ambitious and attainable. To fully realize this potential, we must remain vigilant, intentional, and principled, embracing the opportunities while navigating the uncertainties of this evolving partnership.

In the workplace, AI is anticipated to become integral to organizational strategies, transforming traditional hierarchies and workflows. Startups are already leveraging AI to scale operations with minimal human resources, while larger organizations are exploring ways to integrate AI to unlock new efficiencies. This shift suggests a move towards more fluid, project-based models where AI acts as a connector, and human roles focus on coordination and strategic oversight. (WIRED)

The creative industries are also experiencing significant transformations due to AI integration. Generative AI models are assisting in tasks ranging from content creation to design, enabling creatives to explore new styles and compositions. While AI can handle routine aspects of creative work, human creativity remains essential for intricate and high-value tasks, suggesting a future where AI serves as a collaborative tool that enhances human creativity rather than replacing it. (Financial Times)

In healthcare, AI's role is expanding beyond diagnostics to include personalized treatment plans and patient monitoring. AI-driven tools can analyze vast datasets to identify patterns and predict health outcomes, supporting medical professionals in making informed decisions. This collaboration aims to improve patient care by combining AI's analytical capabilities with human empathy and clinical expertise.

However, the increasing integration of AI into various sectors raises concerns about overdependence. Relying too heavily on AI systems can lead to vulnerabilities, such as systemic failures in the event of technological malfunctions or cyberattacks. Additionally, overreliance on AI may result in the erosion of essential human skills, as individuals become accustomed to deferring decisions to machines. To mitigate these risks, it is crucial to maintain a balance where AI serves as an aid to human decision-making rather than a replacement.

Ethical considerations also play a significant role in the future of human-AI collaboration. Ensuring that AI systems are designed and implemented with fairness, transparency, and accountability is essential to prevent biases and maintain public trust. Collaborative efforts between technologists, ethicists, and policymakers are necessary to establish guidelines that promote responsible AI use.

Looking ahead, the evolution of human-AI collaboration will depend on continuous learning and adaptation. Both humans and AI systems must evolve, with humans developing new skills to work effectively alongside AI, and AI systems being designed to learn from human feedback. This mutual learning approach can lead to more effective collaborations, where the strengths of both humans and AI are leveraged to achieve common goals.

In conclusion, the future of human-AI collaboration holds immense potential to transform various sectors by enhancing efficiency, driving innovation, and addressing complex challenges. However, realizing this potential requires careful consideration of ethical implications, efforts to prevent overdependence, and a commitment to fostering mutual learning between humans and AI system.

Emerging Trends in Artificial Intelligence

Artificial intelligence (AI) is no longer confined to the realm of futuristic speculation; it has permeated our lives in profound and often subtle ways, reshaping industries, influencing decisions, and redefining how humans interact with the digital world. As the field continues to evolve, emerging trends in AI are setting the stage for transformative changes that will challenge established paradigms and expand the boundaries of possibility.

One of the most significant developments in artificial intelligence is the transition from narrowly specialized systems to models with greater contextual understanding. These systems are moving toward an enhanced capacity to interpret the nuances of human expression, intent, and emotion. The shift from task-specific algorithms to versatile frameworks is unlocking potential for machines to function in more integrative and adaptive roles, capable of participating in intricate decision-making processes alongside humans. This evolution is not merely a technical milestone but a step toward a deeper synthesis of artificial and human intelligence.

The sophistication of generative AI represents another major leap forward. With the advent of advanced models, the creative potential of artificial systems has expanded dramatically. These technologies are redefining creative workflows, enabling the production of art, literature, and music that challenges traditional notions of originality and authorship. However, the growing presence of generative systems also raises questions about intellectual property, authenticity, and the ethical implications of synthetic creativity. As society grapples with these issues, a nuanced understanding of how to integrate these tools meaningfully will be critical.

In parallel, the increasing convergence of AI with edge computing is transforming how and where intelligence is deployed. Decentralized processing enables AI systems to operate in real-time within devices, removing the dependency on centralized cloud infrastructures. This trend is particularly impactful in areas such as autonomous mobility, industrial automation, and personalized healthcare. By embedding intelligence closer to the point of action, these systems offer unprecedented responsiveness and a more seamless integration into everyday experiences.

AI's evolution also reflects a growing emphasis on systems designed to mimic and support human reasoning. The aspiration is not to replicate cognition but to create models capable of interpreting complex environments in ways that align with human values and priorities. These systems are increasingly being tailored to facilitate ethical decision-making, address inequities, and prioritize inclusivity. The intentional integration of fairness and accountability into AI frameworks is not merely a technical endeavor; it is a testament to the importance of embedding humanity's collective aspirations into its creations.

Perhaps most intriguing is the potential of AI to redefine how societies understand collaboration. Artificial intelligence is not only a tool to augment individual capacities but a force that can bridge divides—geographical, cultural, and intellectual—by facilitating communication and creating new platforms for shared understanding. In areas like education, these systems are fostering opportunities for tailored learning environments that accommodate diverse perspectives, enabling individuals to engage with knowledge in ways that resonate with their unique contexts.

Yet, the rapid proliferation of AI also underscores the growing necessity for vigilance. The emerging capabilities of these systems highlight the dual-edged nature of innovation. The misuse of advanced algorithms for misinformation, surveillance, and exploitation underscores the need for safeguards that are as advanced as the systems themselves. The path forward demands a collective commitment to foresight, responsibility, and collaboration among researchers, policymakers, and communities to shape AI's trajectory responsibly.

Artificial intelligence is no longer defined solely by its capacity to automate; it is evolving into a collaborator, a creator, and a conduit for profound transformation. The trends shaping its development reflect a discipline increasingly focused on embedding empathy, understanding, and ethical alignment within its designs. These advancements herald a future where intelligence, whether human or artificial, is not measured solely by capability but by its capacity to enrich the lives it touches and the world it seeks to enhance.

Preparing for an ai-enhanced tomorrow, as artificial intelligence weaves itself more intricately into the fabric of society, preparing for an AI-enhanced future requires more than technological expertise; it demands a thoughtful reimagining of our collective aspirations, values, and priorities. The promise of a tomorrow shaped by artificial systems is not merely about efficiency or innovation. It is about creating an environment where human potential flourishes alongside the advancements of intelligent machines, fostering a world that is not only smarter but also profoundly more connected.

Central to this vision is the need to cultivate adaptability and curiosity. As AI evolves, it challenges traditional ways of thinking and disrupts established norms. Embracing this dynamic landscape calls for an openness to uncharted possibilities and a willingness to engage in lifelong learning. It is not merely about acquiring knowledge but about nurturing an attitude of exploration, where the unknown becomes an invitation rather than a threat. This mindset ensures that individuals are not just passengers in this evolving narrative but active participants shaping its course.

The workplaces of tomorrow will be characterized by symbiotic interactions between humans and intelligent systems. Rather than reducing opportunities, AI presents a chance to redefine what it means to contribute meaningfully. Repetitive and time-consuming tasks are giving way to opportunities for deeper engagement, allowing for greater emphasis on creativity, empathy, and strategic thinking. This shift invites a reconsideration of how value is measured and encourages environments where collaboration between human insight and machine precision drives innovation forward.

However, preparing for an AI-enhanced future is not solely about technological alignment; it is also a deeply human endeavor. The systems we design reflect our choices, biases, and intentions. Ensuring these creations serve a greater good requires an unwavering commitment to ethical consideration. This means fostering inclusivity, prioritizing equity, and embedding a sense of accountability into every layer of innovation. It is not enough for AI to function; it must also align with the principles that uphold human dignity and fairness.

Education emerges as a cornerstone in this preparation. The next generation will inherit a world where intelligent systems are pervasive, and their ability to thrive will depend on their capacity to navigate this landscape thoughtfully. Beyond technical expertise, fostering critical thinking, empathy, and a global perspective will be paramount. It is these qualities that will enable individuals to not only work alongside intelligent systems but to guide their development in ways that reflect shared human values.

Equally essential is the recognition that preparing for an AI-enhanced tomorrow is a collective effort. No single organization, government, or individual holds all the answers. Collaboration across disciplines, sectors, and borders is vital to ensuring that the benefits of artificial intelligence are distributed equitably. This cooperative spirit must extend beyond innovation to address challenges such as data privacy, misinformation, and the environmental impact of advanced technologies.

As we envision this future, it is important to remember that technology does not exist in isolation. It is shaped by the culture, intentions, and aspirations of the society that builds it. Preparing for an AI-enhanced tomorrow requires a balance between ambition and caution, between the desire to push boundaries and the responsibility to consider consequences. It is a journey not just of progress but of purpose—a chance to reimagine what is possible and to ensure that every step forward reflects the best of what humanity has to offer.

The horizon of an AI-enhanced future is not a distant abstraction; it is an unfolding reality. How we prepare for it will determine whether it becomes a tool for division or a bridge to a more interconnected and harmonious world. This is our opportunity to design not just machines that think but systems that uplift, not just solutions that work but innovations that inspire. The choices made today will shape the essence of tomorrow, reminding us that the heart of any technological journey lies in its ability to illuminate and elevate the human experience.

10 CHAPTER

EMBRACING AI WHILE STAYING HUMAN

As artificial intelligence continues its transformative journey through every corner of human existence, the challenge is not simply to integrate it into our lives but to do so in a way that preserves and amplifies the essence of what it means to be human. Embracing AI is not an act of surrendering control or agency; it is a commitment to harmonize technological ingenuity with the irreplaceable qualities that define our shared humanity—our empathy, creativity, and moral compass.

The rapid ascent of intelligent systems offers unprecedented opportunities to solve complex problems, streamline processes, and extend human capabilities. Yet, this ascent carries with it the imperative to navigate thoughtfully, ensuring that the integration of artificial intelligence does not diminish the human spirit. Machines, regardless of their sophistication, are constructs—tools imbued with purpose and direction by their creators. It is this dynamic that places the responsibility firmly in human hands: to shape AI as a force for good, guided by values that transcend mere functionality.

To embrace AI while staying authentically human, we must cultivate a profound awareness of its duality. It is both a mirror of our intentions and a catalyst for change. Every algorithm reflects the priorities of those who design it, every decision it supports influenced by the data and systems upon which it relies. In this sense, artificial intelligence is not a separate entity but an extension of collective human thought. Its trajectory is determined by the choices we make today—choices that must be rooted in ethical foresight and a long-term vision for the kind of world we wish to create.

This journey demands more than technological fluency; it calls for a renewed focus on the values that bind us together as a species. The embrace of AI must not lead to the erosion of connection, compassion, or cultural richness. Instead, it should enhance these aspects, creating pathways for deeper understanding and collaboration across boundaries. The integration of intelligent systems into education, healthcare, governance, and art offers the potential not only to elevate outcomes but to foster a sense of shared purpose that transcends technological divides.

Humanity's relationship with AI must also be characterized by humility and adaptability. The pursuit of progress should not obscure the need to reflect on its implications, to pause when necessary, and to recalibrate when outcomes deviate from our intentions. AI is a tool, but it is also a teacher, revealing our blind spots, challenging our assumptions, and inspiring us to think more expansively. This iterative dialogue between human and machine holds the potential to elevate both, provided we remain attuned to its lessons.

To stay human in an AI-driven world is not to resist change but to guide it with intention. It is to recognize that intelligence, whether human or artificial, is most powerful when aligned with purpose. The ultimate success of AI will not be measured by its autonomy or efficiency but by its ability to serve humanity's highest aspirations: to heal, to create, to connect, and to understand.

This moment in history is not a crossroads but a convergence, where technology and humanity meet to define what the future will hold. It is an invitation to move forward with courage and conviction, embracing the promise of AI while safeguarding the values that make life meaningful. In this delicate balance lies the essence of progress—not in replacing what makes us human, but in amplifying it. The journey is ours to shape, and the legacy we leave will be determined by our capacity to embrace innovation while remaining steadfastly, unapologetically human.

The Balance Between Technology and Humanity

The relationship between technology and humanity has always been a dynamic interplay, a dance between the progress we seek and the essence of who we are. As innovation accelerates, this balance becomes increasingly delicate, challenging us to harmonize the potential of what we create with the principles that define our existence. The balance between technology and humanity is not a static equilibrium but an ongoing negotiation, one that requires intention, reflection, and an unwavering commitment to prioritize the human experience.

Technology, at its core, is a manifestation of human ingenuity. It reflects our desire to simplify, to explore, to understand. From the first tools crafted to ease labor to the sophisticated algorithms that now shape our interactions, every advancement carries the imprint of human purpose. Yet, the more technology integrates into our lives, the more we must ask what it serves. Does it amplify our connections or isolate us further? Does it foster deeper understanding or encourage passive consumption? These questions form the foundation of the delicate equilibrium we seek to maintain.

At the heart of this balance lies the human element—our empathy, creativity, and moral consciousness. Machines, no matter how advanced, lack the capacity to experience the world as we do. They can simulate decisions, process vast amounts of information, and perform tasks with remarkable efficiency, but they cannot feel the weight of a moral dilemma or appreciate the nuance of a shared moment. It is this irreplaceable human dimension that must guide the integration of technology into our lives. Without it, the risk is not that technology will overpower us, but that we will lose sight of what makes us distinct.

Maintaining this equilibrium requires vigilance, not only in the design of technology but also in how we integrate it into our lives. There is a tendency to defer to the ease and convenience that technology offers, allowing it to dictate the pace and structure of our days. While this can free us from certain burdens, it can also erode our autonomy, fostering a dependency that diminishes our agency. True balance demands a conscious effort to remain engaged, to question the systems we interact with, and to ensure they align with our values rather than merely our desires for comfort or efficiency.

The relationship between humanity and technology also speaks to broader societal dynamics. As artificial intelligence and automation reshape industries, the question is not merely one of economic impact but of cultural and ethical significance. What do we value as a society? What do we prioritize in our communities? These are not technical questions but deeply human ones, and their answers will determine how we navigate this evolving relationship. Technology has the potential to democratize opportunities, bridge divides, and enhance lives, but only if it is directed with purpose and foresight.

Education becomes a critical lever in this dynamic, not just in preparing individuals to navigate a technologically rich environment, but in fostering the qualities that machines cannot replicate. Curiosity, critical thinking, empathy, and ethical reasoning are the cornerstones of maintaining balance. They are the traits that allow us to engage with technology not as passive consumers but as active participants, shaping its trajectory and ensuring it serves a greater good.

The balance between technology and humanity also requires humility. It is easy to marvel at the advancements we create and forget that they are reflections of our own limitations. Technology should not strive to replace human thought or creativity but to extend and enhance them. It is a partner, not an expert, and its value lies not in its independence but in its ability to collaborate with us, to reveal new possibilities without overshadowing the inherent worth of human endeavor.

As we stand at the threshold of an era defined by intelligent systems and pervasive connectivity, the challenge is not merely to integrate these technologies but to infuse them with humanity. This means designing systems that respect privacy, foster inclusivity, and enhance well-being. It means acknowledging the unintended consequences of innovation and addressing them with responsibility and care. It means valuing not just what technology can do but what it should do, guided by principles that prioritize human dignity and flourishing.

The balance between technology and humanity is, ultimately, a reflection of our collective choices. It is a dialogue, a dynamic interplay that will evolve as our capabilities expand and our aspirations deepen. To achieve this balance is not to resist progress but to shape it, to ensure that the tools we create elevate rather than diminish, connect rather than divide, and inspire rather than alienate. It is a journey that calls us to be intentional, thoughtful, and deeply human, even as we push the boundaries of what is possible. In this balance lies not only the future of technology but the essence of what it means to be human in an age of unprecedented possibility.

Building a Symbiotic Relationship with Machines

Building a symbiotic relationship with machines requires a deliberate approach that harmonizes technological advancement with the intricacies of human experience. This relationship is not about subordination or dominance but about fostering a partnership where machines amplify human potential and, in turn, are guided by the ethical and emotional intelligence unique to humanity. As machines evolve, capable of performing tasks that were once the sole domain of human effort, the focus must shift toward collaboration, where both entities contribute to a shared purpose.

At the core of this partnership lies mutual augmentation. Machines excel in areas where precision, scale, and speed are paramount. They can process data at volumes and complexities unimaginable to human cognition, uncovering insights and patterns that fuel innovation. However, these capabilities are sterile without human oversight. The ability to contextualize, interpret, and imbue decisions with empathy and foresight is something no algorithm, regardless of its sophistication, can replicate. It is in this interplay of strengths that true collaboration emerges—a dynamic where human intuition directs machine efficiency toward outcomes that are meaningful and impactful.

This symbiosis also offers an opportunity to redefine the boundaries of creativity. Machines are now contributing to art, music, literature, and design, not as rivals to human creators but as companions in the act of creation. They provide tools and perspectives that can inspire new forms of expression, expanding the horizon of what is artistically possible. Yet, the essence of art—the connection it forges, the emotions it evokes—remains firmly rooted in human experience. This interplay reminds us that technology's role is not to overshadow creativity but to broaden the canvas upon which it is expressed.

Equally significant is how this relationship can address challenges that transcend individual ambition. Machines, when aligned with human values, have the potential to tackle complex global issues, from climate change to public health crises. The efficiency of artificial systems, coupled with human ingenuity, creates opportunities to craft solutions that are both scalable and sustainable. However, this requires machines to operate as more than tools—they must act as extensions of our collective will, designed with accountability and guided by an unwavering commitment to ethical principles.

Trust becomes the linchpin in this partnership. Machines must be designed transparently, allowing people to understand their logic and limitations. It is not enough for systems to function flawlessly; they must also align with the expectations and values of the communities they serve. Trust is cultivated when machines demonstrate reliability without diminishing autonomy, creating an environment where humans feel empowered rather than marginalized by their presence.

This symbiotic relationship also challenges us to reconsider the essence of labor and purpose. As machines take on tasks that are repetitive or data-intensive, they liberate humans to focus on roles that require emotional intelligence, strategic thought, and adaptability. Far from replacing the human element, machines create a space where our unique contributions become more visible and valuable. This shift not only transforms industries but redefines how we measure fulfillment and success, emphasizing impact and creativity over rote efficiency.

For this partnership to thrive, it must be built on a foundation of equity and inclusivity. The benefits of this collaboration should not be confined to a select few but distributed broadly, ensuring that all communities have access to the opportunities it creates. This requires intentional efforts to democratize technology, bridging divides and dismantling barriers that might otherwise exclude marginalized voices from the dialogue. When machines are developed and deployed with inclusivity in mind, they reflect a broader spectrum of perspectives and contribute to a more equitable future.

The relationship between humans and machines is not static; it is an evolving dialogue that will be shaped by the choices we make and the values we uphold. It demands a mindset that values learning and reflection, acknowledging that mistakes will occur, and progress is iterative. It calls for humility in recognizing that while machines are powerful allies, their purpose is to serve humanity, not to supplant it. Above all, it requires a vision rooted in the belief that technology is not an end in itself but a means to enhance the human experience.

Building this symbiotic relationship is one of the defining challenges of our time. It is a call to action, urging us to harness the potential of machines while safeguarding the essence of what makes us human. This partnership, when cultivated thoughtfully, has the capacity to not only transform how we work and live but to elevate the collective aspirations of humanity. It is not a question of whether we will coexist with machines but of how we will shape that coexistence into something that enriches and inspires, leaving a legacy of progress guided by purpose.

Artificial intelligence has evolved from an emerging technology to a fundamental element of our daily lives. Throughout this book, we have explored how AI influences our decisions, transforms our interactions, and reshapes the future of our society. From the conveniences it provides in our homes to its impact on critical sectors like healthcare, education, and work, AI has deeply integrated itself into our existence, shaping it in ways we are only beginning to understand.

However, this progress is not without its challenges. Ethics, privacy, and inequality are crucial issues that must be addressed to ensure this powerful tool is utilized equitably and responsibly. Artificial intelligence not only reflects our values as a society but also has the potential to amplify them—for better or worse. Therefore, dialogue and collaboration among governments, businesses, academics, and citizens are essential in navigating this new era.

Ultimately, how we allow AI to shape our days depends on the choices we make today. With foresight and responsibility, artificial intelligence can become a powerful ally in solving some of humanity's most pressing challenges. This book serves as an invitation to reflect, question, and, above all, actively participate in building a future where technology enhances the best of who we are.

Artificial intelligence is not only shaping our days—it is offering us the opportunity to shape the future. Are we ready to embrace that responsibility?

ABOUT THE AUTHOR

Raúl A.S. Reynoso is a technology enthusiast whose passion for innovation led him to explore the forefront of artificial intelligence. With a background that spans software development, research, and digital strategy, he has spent years studying how AI influences various industries and shapes human experiences. Beyond the tech world, Raúl is a resolute learner who believes in making complex ideas accessible to all. When he's not delving into the latest AI breakthroughs, you can find him traveling, trying out new cuisines, or sharing insights at conferences around the world. *How AI Shapes Our Days* marks his commitment to spark curiosity and dialogue about our rapidly evolving technological landscape.

REFERENCES

1. Gorilla, C. (2024, 13 October). The Impact of AI on Human Creativity - My AI Toolbox. My AI Toolbox. https://myaitoolbox.net/the-impact-of-ai-on-human-creativity/?utm_source=chatgpt.com

2. https://www.theatlantic.com/magazine/archive/2024/11/mcneal-play-akhtar-downey-artificial-intelligence/679949/?utm_source=chatgpt.com

3. Your request has been blocked. This could be due to several reasons. (s. f.). https://www.microsoft.com/en-us/microsoft-365/business-insights-ideas/resources/ai-productivity-tips-business

4. Frommberger, L. (2010). Qualitative spatial abstraction in reinforcement learning., 1-174. https://doi.org/10.1007/978-3-642-16590-0.

5. Legg, S., & Hutter, M. (2007). Universal Intelligence: A Definition of Machine Intelligence. Minds and Machines, 17, 391-444. https://doi.org/10.1007/s11023-007-9079-x.

6. Rodríguez, P. (2023). *Inteligencia artificial: Cómo cambiará el mundo (y tu vida)*. Madrid: Editorial Planeta.

7. Benedict, M., Lee, D., & Roberts, J. (2021). Advances in wearable ECG monitoring and predictive analytics. *Journal of Medical Innovations*, 34(2), 56-72.

8. Mishra, T., Wang, M., & Binnicker, M. J. (2020). Wearable health technology and its role during the COVID-19 pandemic. *Nature Digital Medicine*, 3(1), 156-161.

www.ingramcontent.com/pod-product-compliance
Lightning Source LLC
LaVergne TN
LVHW051338050326
832903LV00031B/3605